AMERICA AT MIDDLE AGE

AMERICA AT MIDDLE AGE

A New History of the United States
in the Twentieth Century

Louis Galambos

New Press

McGraw-Hill Book Company
New York   St. Louis   San Francisco
Hamburg   Mexico   Toronto

1 2 3 4 5 6 7 8 9 DOCDOC 8 7 6 5 4 3

ISBN 0-07-022682-2

LIBRARY OF CONGRESS CATALOGING IN PUBLICATION DATA

Galambos, Louis.
America at middle age.
1. United States—20th century. I. Title.
E741.G34   973.9   82-7806
ISBN 0-07-022682-2   AACR2

Book design by Janice Willcocks Stern

To my talented daughters, Denise and Jenny. They helped ease their father into his golden middle years.

Contents

1

MIDDLE AGE CREEPS UP
ON AMERICA

You saw him on a street corner last weekend wearing a new warm-up suit and a pair of expensive running shoes. The shoes were spotless. He was jogging in place, waiting for the light to change. He looked grim. Jogging was serious business, and he seemed determined to win the war he had just declared on the fat around his waist. He was sweating. Limping slightly. He was middle-aged.

Perhaps you were the jogger. Or his wife—equally sore, equally middle-aged, equally serious about not letting things get any worse than they are. If you were out there in your new running shoes, you probably recall rather clearly how good you felt a few years ago. Then you were that leaner person who is still there, inside your body, waiting to come out when the diet is successful, the jogging has firmed up those muscles, and an extra set of tennis has helped to put life back in order. The sense of order—just like the image of a smaller, leaner you—is left over from an earlier day when your life was less complicated than it is today, when there were a few obvious goals to achieve, when you were still very certain that you could meet your own high standards of performance.

1

If you were the jogger or if you just understand how he feels, then you also understand something important about the United States today. America is a middle-aged nation. The country has built up some extra fat around the waist and become aware of late that neither its cardiovascular system nor its sense of purpose is quite as strong as it used to be. Every so often Americans seem determined to do something about the shape their country is in. When these fits coincide with a presidential election, the voters vent their distress on the party in power. But the symptoms of middle age persist. New leaders proclaim new policies and reaffirm the national values, but we somehow fail to recapture that energy and sense of direction that characterized the country in an earlier day.

Clearly the United States once stood for certain ideals and accomplished certain ends that gave a special meaning to the national experience. Democracy, individualism, and revolutionary dissent from tyranny were part of that tradition. A young American nation produced political documents that gave lasting expression to these ideals and created new political institutions that gave most of its citizens an opportunity to select their leaders and to influence the policies they implemented. America took in millions of immigrants, subdued a wilderness, and built an economic order that made our standard of living the envy of the world.

But today those accomplishments seem threatened, the ideals tarnished. Our democratic government is overgrown with shortsighted interest groups that hover over the legislatures, cling to our executives, and clog the judicial process. Even when we applaud the objectives of one of these groups (the one we happen to belong to), its activities often leave us worried about the manner in which public policy is framed and implemented. As individuals, however, we seem helpless. We feel overwhelmed by the giant bureaucracies that send us computerized bills, that decide what the people in Akron,

Ohio, should be doing about their athletic programs, that spend millions of dollars as casually as we buy a pizza on Friday night.

What do these millions buy us? We always seem to be on the wrong side, the losing side, when there is a revolution anywhere in the world. We have just about completed our magnificent interstate highway system but we may not be able to use it in the summer because we cannot afford the gasoline. Both Exxon and the U.S. Department of Energy have played important roles in the political economy of the nation, but their claims to our allegiance have been weakened by the events of the recent past. Americans who are straining to pay their gasoline and utility bills are understandably suspicious of institutions such as these. Although our standard of living is still high, our income is threatened by continuing inflation and by the concerted action of a group of oil-producing nations that we have always treated with contempt or merely ignored. In the past, we could afford to ignore them. Americans had more of everything than we needed. More oil. More iron and steel. More food. Now it appears that we are losing that advantage and may actually be falling behind.

Like our friend the jogger, however, we are still armed with a vision. We know what the nation's ideals have been and what its accomplishments were. The lean America of an earlier day beckons. We can recapture the past. We can select new leaders who will know how to run things. We can trim down the bureaucracy. Chop away the regulations. Reaffirm our distinctive values. Restore in our people a firm sense of purpose, in our polity a measure of responsibility, in our economy a desire for competition and achievement. Or so it seems.

The leaders we have chosen have been mindful of these middle-aged longings. President Ronald Reagan proclaimed in his inaugural address the beginning of "an era of national renewal." We could, he said, "renew our determination, our courage, and our strength. Let us renew our faith and our hope. We have every right to dream heroic dreams." His predecessor, Jimmy Carter, had expressed a similar faith at his inaugural. "The American dream endures," he said. "We must once again have full faith in our country—and in one another." Then, "America can be better. We can be even stronger than before." In the mid-sixties Lyndon Johnson put his rhetoric at the service of this theme, reminding us that earlier Americans "made a covenant with this land. Conceived in justice, written in liberty, bound in union, it was meant one day to inspire the hopes of all mankind, and it binds us still. If we keep its terms, we shall flourish." If we succeeded, Johnson said, it would be "not because of what we own, but rather because of what we believe." During the 1950s, Dwight D. Eisenhower also exploited the renewal theme when he established a presidential commission to appraise "the potentials of our future." As the commission's final report made clear, the nation's "paramount goal" had been enunciated long ago in the Declaration of Independence. "Our enduring aim is to build a nation and help build a world in which every human being shall be free to develop his capacities to the fullest. We must rededicate ourselves to this principle," the report urged, and in cooperation with other "free peoples of the world," we would be able to "develop unmatched strength and vindicate the mighty vision of the Declaration."

These are typical obsessions of early middle age: the recovery of strength; the reaffirmation of a vision that long had served to guide life but has somehow been neglected of late; the need to rededicate one's life, to rekindle the faith. To believe was thus to become. America would then be certain and strong, like the lean, tough country that had first proclaimed this faith and had then put its principles into practice. The desire to recapture a past sense of purpose and to recover strength is what brings the middle-aged jogger onto the streets, pushing through the pain that reminds him that faith alone may not free him from the burdens he has accumulated over the years. The United States has had its own share of painful episodes in recent years, but like the jogger, the nation is still determined to push through, to become "better," to become "even stronger than before."

II

But can a nation really be middle-aged as a person is? The United States seems to resemble a sweating, overweight jogger, and a glance at the front page of almost any newspaper provides reminders that America has changed in ways that leave us uncomfortable, if not angry. Nevertheless, we know that societies do not age in exactly the same way that we do. You and I have a biological life cycle. We have a youth that is followed by inevitable physical changes. Give or take a few years, we all slip into middle age at about the same time, and physiologists can predict what will happen to us with a degree of accuracy that is as encouraging to their profession as it is dismaying to most of us. Their trend lines all point toward the same conclusion. If we are fortunate, we will get old. Then—give or take a few years—the cycle will end.

Even the psychology of aging follows a fairly regular path. In the last few years scholars have made considerable progress in charting the common patterns of ideas and activities that characterize adult life. We have learned much about the emotions of early adulthood, about the rocky transition to middle age, about the less traumatic but more threatening glide into old age. Even the confrontation with death has been studied and shown to yield those normal psychological paths that delight the social scientists and leave us grumpy about losing our individuality—and in this case our lives.

Nations face no such inexorable cycle. They are not organisms. It is not inevitable that one phase will follow another, that underlying changes will turn the youthful society into a middle-aged country, and then into an aged nation. Societies do not face extinction—at least not in the same way that we do.

So much for the differences. There still remains enough similarity between the person and the nation to suggest that the idea of aging can help us understand our recent past and some of the problems that are bothering Americans today. We have, after all, grown used to talking about the early United States as a young country. The bicentennial celebrations were full of such references. So are our history textbooks. Associated in our minds with the idea of youth is the concept of rapid growth. The young nation, like a child, experiences rapid growth in population. The average citizen is relatively young (as was certainly the case in the nineteenth-century United States). The economy also grows rapidly and experiences the sort of major transitions we associate with youth. There are in the young nation fewer barriers to change; the people can experiment more freely, in part because their institutions are less settled and the burden of tradition is relatively light.

In the American case the rapid growth was geographical as well as economic. We had a physical frontier. Americans pressed across the continent, transforming a small, weak republic on the periphery of the European market system into a great power with abundant natural resources and a large population. In the course of that expansion, Americans committed acts of aggression that seem from our present vantage point to be at the very least embarrassing. They pushed aside the Indians, and many Americans find it uncomfortable to have the descendants of these Indians around today to remind us of that aspect of our heritage. The Mexican-American War yielded a similar bounty, as did the brief and successful war with Spain. The latter struggle left us in control of an unruly population in the Philippines, but the United States

Army subdued those people in much the same way that it had earlier handled the Indians.

The concept of youth, a young nation, helps us excuse these episodes in our history. The leaders of young nations can be expected to act rashly—can even be excused their aggressive acts. The people of a young, growing nation of course exerted pressure on their leaders to fulfill their dreams—to seek expansion, to foster economic growth, to uphold the nation's honor. Popular leaders met these demands. From John Adams to Theodore Roosevelt, our presidents frequently yielded to the public desire for such policies. Roosevelt was perhaps the most famous for championing these popular goals, and it is appropriate that we still identify Teddy with a child's stuffed animal. He was the young and vigorous spokesman for a nation that followed at least half of his advice about speaking softly and carrying a big stick.

When we label the United States as a young nation, we are comparing it—sometimes consciously—with countries we recognize as old. The first contrast that usually occurs to me is with China. Who comes to mind when you think of China? For many of us the image is that of a very old, white-bearded man with a thoughtful expression on his face; he personifies a nation in which traditional patterns of life persist, outliving all of the dynasties, invasions, and revolutions, even the most recent one. In spite of new governments and technological advances, the long-established patterns of social and economic life give way grudgingly in China. The ancient Asian society and the young United States of the nineteenth century present a contrast in almost every regard. Even after the communist revolution in China and the emergence of a new political order, the social matrix of a traditional peasant society has resisted change in a manner alien to America's experience.

When we compare the United States to the European nations, a similar if less decisive contrast emerges. What

American can fail to be impressed by the great age of the European societies? My own university, Johns Hopkins, recently celebrated its one hundredth anniversary. But a century ago, when Johns Hopkins was founded, the University of Paris was already more than six hundred years old. Oxford was six hundred years old before the American colonies won their independence, and the University of Bologna was conferring degrees long before Columbus discovered the New World. In all of these European institutions, traditions are far more deeply rooted than they are in even the oldest American universities.

Thus it is with many aspects of life in Europe and America. On the Continent we see churches that predate our first colonies, families that trace their lineage back through more generations than most of us can imagine, and villages that have resisted modernization and preserved a culture that neither the automobile nor the railroad—nor for that matter radio and television—have been able to reshape. In England, too, Americans find everywhere the reminders of just how young our society is. By English standards, our oldest communities are still new cities and our folkways fairly recent innovations.

Noting these differences, historian Louis Hartz told us some years ago that America's uniqueness as a society was grounded primarily in the fact that this country had no feudal past. As a new society, our history was truncated. There had been no feudal institutions to rebel against. Thus the United States did not develop either a strong radical left (which arose in Europe out of the fight against those feudal interests) or a vocal, reactionary right (which defended them). Our spectrum of political ideas was narrow and relatively liberal because we were a new, a very young society.

Hartz's insight was important and his analysis of our political ideas rang true for the period before the present century. But we need to reconsider this subject from the vantage point of the 1980s. My contention is that our basic institutions have changed in decisive ways in the present century. America has not suddenly become an ancient, traditional society, but it is also no longer a young nation. The appropriate metaphor is that of a country entering middle age and experiencing problems that can be understood better if we will compare our society with an individual making the ofttimes rocky transition to midlife.

III

One of the lessons that current psychologists have taught us is that this particular transition will be most painful when an individual is unable to adjust his or her self-image to the realities of middle age. Similarly with the United States, the failure to understand that ours is no longer the young nation of the early nineteenth century can create problems. Our recent history suggests that for many Americans such adjustments will be slow in coming and will follow prolonged and futile efforts to recapture a youth that has passed. This helps explain the popularity of the renewal theme in our presidential rhetoric and popular magazines. Recall, too, how difficult it was for Americans to give up the image of a society consisting primarily of yeoman farmers. Long after we were largely an urban, industrial society, the image of the pioneer, the self-sufficient plowman, lingered on and diverted our attention from the realities of our city-centered life. Other remnants of our youth have enjoyed a similar longevity. We have, for instance, continued to consider ourselves the advocates of national revolutions—this despite the fact that we repeatedly and forcefully attempt to crush such movements throughout the world. We have also clung to individualistic values more appropriate to the fast-expanding, atomistic economy of the nineteenth century than they are to the type of mature, corporate economy we have today.

The images of youth persist. Their powerful hold suggests that America's midlife crisis will be long and painful. No matter how long we try, however, we will not be able to will away the realities of middle life any more than our friend on the street corner will be able to jog his way back into youth. Maybe the best thing we can do now is to look at some of those realities, charting some of the social trends that have shaped America's recent past and will perforce dominate its immediate future.

2

THE AGING PROCESS

When you drive across the George Washington Bridge, you seldom give much thought to the age and strength of the structure. Busy trying to stay in the proper lane, you don't worry about the cables and massive pillars, all of which seem ageless. The paint peels off, but the bridge itself has the permanence of the shoreline.

To the metallurgist, however, the cables and girders of a bridge seem anything but permanent and ageless. He sees the metal slowly changing as stress alters the internal properties of the steel. Eventually even the strongest girder has to be replaced. The metal ages, becomes more brittle. It can no longer support the weight of the structure. The bridge engineer sees just this sort of silent process of change taking place in the base of the bridge, and a geologist will tell us that even the rocks of the shoreline are aging as the wind and waves slowly wear at their surface.

Similar changes take place in nations, and the most significant of these developments often pass unnoticed as we go about our daily business. Nervous about staying in our particular lane of life, we pay little attention to the changes I have in mind, most of which fail to make the front page of our newspaper. They take place too slowly to be news. They occur beneath the surface of events that holds our attention. They are not the product of a single decision, are seldom the theme of a presidential address or the subject of a congressional inquiry. These slow, incremental changes alter our society in decisive ways, but the results accumulate over such a long period of time that we seldom give them a thought.

While we disregard these quiet, long-term trends, they transform our society just as surely as erosion reshapes the riverbank and stress ages the girders of a bridge. Eventually we all come to see that our society has changed. Then, frequently long after the fact, we want someone to do something about what has happened; at that moment, as if by magic, our national leaders will start to make speeches that express the renewal theme. Sometimes these speeches are soothing to us. They do not, however, identify with any clarity the sources of our discontent, and they certainly do not help us figure out what exactly might be done to improve conditions. Today, I think, we badly need to achieve a deeper understanding of the major changes that have taken place in the United States in this century. What, then, has actually happened to transform America and leave so many of us disturbed?

II

There are three fundamental changes that must be understood before we can correctly analyze our modern institutions and current mood of discontent. The first of these is the geographical aspect of America's middle age. Over the first three centuries of our history, expansion continually renewed the frontier, adding fresh resources to fuel our economic growth. We acquired at very little cost (in either men or money) a vast continental empire that barely could be settled before the end of the nineteenth century. Without heavy immigration—especially during the decades following 1840—the process of settlement would have been much delayed. With help from those Old World countries that allowed America to drain off their excess populations, we were able by 1890 to fill out the great continental domain we acquired by a combination of force and astute diplomatic maneuvering.

Before we praise too strongly the men who devised that diplomacy, it is important to remember that they were blessed with certain advantages that our present-day leaders no longer have. One was America's insignificance. The country that obsesses us was, after all, just a minor way station to the great European powers. They could dump their excess people on the American prairies. They could look to America for the food that would provision their more lucrative colonies. But the crucial questions of international affairs all involved the other European nations. Had North America been more important to the British, the colonies could never have won their independence when they did. Later, the young nation acquired vast lands rich in natural resources for much the same reason. The European powers were concerned elsewhere, and our own immediate neighbors were too weak to resist our aggressive expansion. We pushed forcefully to the Pacific Ocean and then spent several decades settling the land we had acquired.

At that point in our history—in the late nineteenth century—the United States faced an important fork in the road. Down one side of the fork ran a path that was earnestly favored by those Americans who wanted to see the country continue its expansion overseas. According to these advocates of empire, we should acquire the bases we needed to defend ourselves and, as an added bonus, new markets for our goods and new sources of raw materials. These arguments were appealing to many Americans, and the spokesmen for empire succeeded for a time. The United States acquired Hawaii, Puerto Rico, and, temporarily, the Philippines, as a result of our successful prosecution of the war with Spain.

But during these same years, the United States was also exploring the other path, experimenting with policies designed to achieve some of the same results as conquest in a more moderate fashion. In our journey down that other fork of the road, we called for an open door for American traders in China; we began to oversee the financial affairs of Latin American countries within our sphere of influence; we used our capital to implement policies that were labeled Dollar Diplomacy. In brief, the United States used its political and economic power to press for advantages in its relations abroad. Giant corporations like United Fruit and Standard Oil often profited from these efforts, as did many smaller American firms. The U.S. impinged on the sovereignty of other nations in order to keep markets open for its companies and to assure that America could draw upon these countries for particular raw materials. Without incurring the price of carving out and maintaining colonies, we hoped thus to gain many of the political and economic advantages that the traditional type of empire would have provided us.

Ours would be a distinctly American style of commercial empire—loosely defined, subjected to conflicting pressures from domestic interest groups, frequently altered in form as well as substance. The boundaries of our new domain were vague largely because the U.S. stake overseas was for many decades so small. Neither exports nor imports were a very large element in our total business activity. To particular firms that had substantial investments overseas, public support for their private efforts could be vital; but it was no simple matter to persuade either the State Department or the president to act on their behalf. For every company or industry helped in this way, there was likely to be another company, a political faction, or an ethnic group whose interests would be damaged. Our political leaders continually responded to these pressures at home and to shifts in the international balance of power. As a result, the U.S. commercial empire took shape in fits and starts.

Still, there was in the years before the First World War much to be said for this policy. At times it appeared to be cumbersome and costly, as was the case, for instance, when our marines had to move into Latin countries to ensure that they would behave in what we felt was a proper manner. But, for the most part, the commercial empire was cheap and successful. By contrast, further expansion through conquest became unpalatable to most Americans. Conquest overseas— unlike the conquest of California—clashed with our ideals and caused thorny constitutional problems. We abruptly stopped our trek down that fork of the road. In fact we retraced our steps, gradually withdrawing from most, but not all, of our colonial outposts. As we did, the preservation of our commercial empire became the central economic policy of American foreign relations in this century.

From our perspective today, we can see why such a choice was reasonable. In the years 1900–1917 much of the world could still be penetrated by determined American traders and by the multinational corporations that were just beginning to emerge in this country. Frequently the government was able to support these commercial ventures (although seldom with as much force as American businessmen felt was needed). In those days we could flex our military and economic muscles and anticipate that the weaker nations would soon find a way to give us most of what we wanted. Commercial penetration along these lines finessed most of the difficult constitutional, moral, and international problems created by conquest. Americans had, it seemed, found a better way, certainly a cheaper way, to achieve their economic objectives overseas.

As it turned out, however, America had barely opted for commercial empire before major changes around the world began to threaten that policy. Over the years since 1917, the forces of nationalism and socialist revolution have dramatically altered one country after another and gradually closed off substantial parts of the world to our businessmen. Wherever the revolutionary process and nationalistic aspirations took hold, they altered the country's economic relations with the United States. We could often continue to do business with those parts of the world, but now our relations were shaped primarily by their long-term needs and governmental policies, not by the immediate demands of American businessmen. All too frequently the United States found itself negotiating just to achieve equality, not dominance. Thus the United States slowly and grudgingly was forced to back away from the powerful position it had held at the turn of the century.

The commercial empire became in effect a kind of holding action. Understanding that aspect of our history helps us see why we have since the early 1900s opposed the revolutions that threatened to erode our international economic position. From the Russian Revolution to the present day, the United States has been using its power in an effort to block these threatening developments. While most Americans think of their country as a liberal nation, the friend of nationalistic self-expression, most of the world correctly sees us as the opponent of the most significant social movements taking place in their parts of the world. The U.S. policy of containment, in this broad sense, does not date from the late 1940s. America has been trying to contain the most powerful forces of change in international affairs for most of this century.

The contrast between our history before 1900 and after that date could hardly be more complete. From the colonial period through the end of the nineteenth century, Americans aggressively expanded their territorial domain. In the present century, the United States stopped growing geographically, sought to stabilize a far-reaching capitalist order, and then was forced to give way, step by step, as nationalistic and revolutionary movements chipped away at the frontiers of our economic realm.

In this geographic sense we are a middle-aged society struggling not to grow but to hang on to a position achieved many years ago. The United States reminds me of a fifty-year-old manager of a branch plant who finds his career blocked. He cannot bring himself to take the risks of looking for another job, and is prudent not to try. All that he can do is protect what he has by trying to fend off the assaults of younger, more aggressive executives who aspire to his job. This harsh picture is difficult to accept—especially in light of America's liberal past and its historic role in the development of the Western democratic tradition. But ignoring these aspects of our relationship to a changing world leaves us unable to explain to ourselves most of the leading characteristics of our own international relations. That brand of self-deception can be as dangerous to the middle-aged nation as it is to the middle-aged executive.

III

It helps a bit to be honest, to acknowledge that geographically the United States has entered its middle years and to recognize that the same sort of change has taken place in our population. This demographic transition—like the geopolitical shift—took place slowly, unevenly, and without great fanfare. During the early phases of America's history, the population of this country experienced an astonishing rate of natural increase. The rate was unusually high by European standards. Americans of that time had very large families. In an agricultural society which offered numerous opportunities to acquire land, a large family provided the extra hands that were needed to work the crops. Accompanying the high birth rate was a relatively low rate of mortality. Life in the new country was, on balance, healthier than it had been in England or on the Continent. Owing to natural increase and to immigration, the American population—a distinctly youthful population—doubled in size every twenty to twenty-five years during the eighteenth century.

The great century of the immigrant was, however, the nineteenth. Then the people came in great waves, created both by pushes from their motherlands and by the pull of economic opportunity in the new country. The first such major wave brought the Irish in the 1840s and 1850s; successive waves gave America its distinctive German immigrants, followed by southern and eastern Europeans (including one of my grandfathers). Between 1840 and 1920 immigration added about thirty-three million people to an American population that was continuing to increase by over twenty-six percent each decade.

The contribution of the immigrants was particularly important during the nineteenth century because the rate of natural increase in the United States population was then beginning to decline. Americans were by that time having smaller families. In the urban areas where more and more of the people lived, a large family was no longer an economic asset. Even in settled agricultural areas there was good cause to have a smaller family and thus avoid the problems of deciding how to divide an estate that consisted primarily of a single farm. In the late nineteenth century these conditions became even more pronounced, and by 1900 the birth rate was only about half of what it had been in 1800.

The long-term decline in the birth rate has continued—with one significant interruption—through the twentieth century. The 1940s produced a much-heralded baby boom, but that decade was the exception that proves the rule. Over the years Americans have been having smaller and smaller families. The average age of the population has increased. More women have decided not to have children at all. By the

1970s the birth rate in our society was only one-third of the 1800 rate. The figures are impressive: in 1800 there had been fifty-five live births per 1,000 persons in the population; by 1900, only thirty-two; and by 1970 only eighteen. In their private lives, Americans were making decisions about their families that were gradually changing the basic nature of our society. As late as 1914, however, the total effect of those decisions on the population still seemed negligible because immigrants were continuing to pour into this country—about one and a quarter million entered the United States in that year alone.

Then the First World War suddenly stopped the flow of people to North America, and Congress in 1924 made that condition relatively permanent by passing "an Act to limit the immigration of aliens into the United States. . . ." The law worked. The number of immigrants entering the country was sharply reduced and has stayed low to the present day. The motives for deciding to choke off immigration in this way were varied, as they always are with any important piece of federal legislation. However, my interest here is not in discerning the motives for taking this momentous step. My concern is with the results of the decision, which were immediate, obvious, and significant. The growth rate of the country's population fell off sharply and has since that date remained relatively low and stable. The political decision of 1924 thus complemented the private decisions that Americans had long been making about the size of their families.

Through contraception and Congress, Americans had opted for a more stable population. For our purposes, the most important aspect of these decisions was the manner in which they coincided with the other major watershed we have discussed—that is, the end of the nation's geographical expansion. As America's long phase of growth was coming to an end, its people decided they could no longer tolerate an unrestrained growth in population. What could be more reasonable? In that way the existing balance between natural resources and labor would be maintained. The dynamic, youthful years of unrestrained immigration and large families were over. A mature society with an older population had chosen a new pattern of growth, one more consistent with its stable frontiers.

IV

At this point you should be able to guess what the third fundamental change was. As our population leveled off and our frontiers became more stable, the American economy had to adjust to these new conditions. Our entire economic system changed in some very basic ways. Most of us sense this. We read the newspaper, watch TV, and reflect on our own careers. We know our economy is different than it used to be. But still it is hard to see exactly what has changed. We know, for instance, that American capitalism has long been founded on the idea of competing in order to achieve economic success. Tomorrow at the office you may be reminded subtly that this has not changed and that ours is still a competitive society. The threat of failure is right there, just beneath the surface. But then you read about the government's plans to bail out another giant corporation that is faced with bankruptcy, and you wonder: "What, exactly, has happened? Why is the federal government using my money to prevent a poorly managed private company from failing?" More doubts creep in when you buy your first foreign car. When you notice that the economy has sagged into recession but that prices are still going up. When you realize that you are earning more money this year than you thought you ever would make but you are still falling behind, unable to keep up with the rate of inflation, not really as well off as you were a few years ago.

The easiest way to resolve all of these doubts is to blame

the government. Some years ago it was popular to blame the Russians for all of our problems. Before that there were Americans who thought our economic difficulties could be traced to England, or to the money power in Wall Street, or to a Zionist conspiracy. Some still do. But alas, our economic quandary can not be tracked to the doorstep of some foreign power or even to the front stoop of the White House.

Whether we like it or not, our economic system has in the past century experienced a fundamental change. For most of its history, America has been a country blessed with unusual natural resources; relative to these resources, America has been chronically short of both capital and labor. Think for a moment about the situation faced by the early settlers in the New World. They had for the taking more land and other resources than they could profitably exploit. Not until the colonies had more hands to work the fields and more capital to finance these endeavors could they begin to make full use of their resources. But by that time, another frontier to the west beckoned, and the cycle was repeated again and again. Only in the last century has the balance between resources, capital, and labor changed decisively. Between 1880 and 1980, America gradually became a nation with more capital and more people than its own natural resources can profitably employ. In that regard we have become more like the other leading industrial powers of the world. We are no longer a young nation filling out an unexplored, unexploited continent. We are, in economic terms, a middle-aged nation trying to learn the best way to use land and other resources whose limits can be seen.

When this transition in our economic life began, the changes were at first barely noticeable. In 1890, the government announced that there no longer was a physical frontier, an area that was (by the standards of the census bureau) still unsettled. But who could worry about this turning point when even American agriculture was continuing to expand? The number of farms continued to grow, as did the number of acres under cultivation. When at last (around 1920) the agricultural system began to level off and even when the number of farms and farm families settled into a long, downward trend, there seemed to be no real reason for concern. There were still other types of frontiers, other abundant resources waiting to be exploited.

The son of a farmer could go to the state agricultural and mechanical college and use his training not to build up the farm—as those who had planned these institutions hoped he would—but to escape the countryside. He might, for instance, find employment in one of those industries exploiting the nation's rich mineral reserves. At the turn of the century, too, the lumber industry was just beginning to slash through the magnificent forests of the Northwest. There were also southern pines to harvest. In the South there were large deposits of iron ore and coal that were being brought into production, resources that offered opportunities to the young man fleeing the farm and to the businessman's son who had perhaps inherited some capital and a flair for entrepreneurship.

They might look to the Southwest, where at the turn of the century fortunes had already been made in lumber, and the discovery of seemingly unlimited sources of oil and gas promised to bankroll a new class of millionaires. The manner in which the Gulf Coast oil deposits were developed in those years is interesting (particularly to those of us who have had problems paying our gasoline bills lately). In Texas in the early 1900s, new wells were brought in so fast that frequently there were no storage tanks to hold the crude oil; often the producers dug deep trenches that were used to hold the extra oil until tank cars and storage tanks were available. While much oil was wasted, there was no incentive to conserve it. The oil belonged to the first person who could pump it out of the ground, and the producer who waited merely would be giving his oil to those other owners who were draining it out of the same field. It was better to recover half of your oil than to lose all of it to a competitor.

Even with the tremendous waste of the early years of southwestern oil development, the industry was so lucrative, the profits were so great, that the industry's largest corporation—the giant Standard Oil Company—could not bring the situation under control. Under John D. Rockefeller's firm guidance, Standard Oil had in the 1880s and 1890s acquired control of about ninety percent of the nation's oil industry. But the new fields on the Gulf Coast undercut his near-monopoly. New companies sprang up to challenge Standard's market power. New family fortunes were built up as southwestern entrepreneurs tapped the region's greatest natural resource.

This type of rapid, extensive development, wasteful of resources but highly profitable, continued the tradition set in the previous three centuries of American expansion. In agriculture, we had skinned the land: farmed out the fertility of the soil and then moved on to new and more productive land. In lumber we had cut and slashed the forests, wasting all but those trees that were most profitable to turn into lumber. In mining the story was the same; our methods had been suited to a nation rich in natural resources but short of labor and capital.

Who could fault the results of three centuries of extensive economic development along these lines? The United States was by 1900 the largest and wealthiest nation in the world. We had lost our insignificance! Our gross national product exceeded that of every country on the European continent. The U.S. economy was almost twice the size of Great Britain's. We had by 1900 left in our dust the nation that had originally colonized America. We had, moreover, kept our income per capita very high despite a rate of population growth that exceeded that of any other nation in the Western world.

Indeed, our high standard of living was the magnet that drew those millions of immigrants to the U.S.

During America's first three centuries of growth, our economy had, like a rising tide, carried the population upward toward greater prosperity. While the tide's progress was uneven—there were deep depressions as well as phases of very rapid expansion—and while some were washed aside and others washed under, the long-term results of our extensive growth were on the average highly favorable. Over a lifetime of effort, most Americans accumulated greater wealth. The distribution of wealth was very uneven. The myth of rags to riches was for the vast majority just that, a myth. But over these three centuries, the tide of economic growth gradually carried most Americans to higher levels of income and wealth. If the great bulk of the population seemed satisfied with the way things were done in the United States, there was good hard evidence in their own family's history to justify that satisfaction.

Since the beginning of the present century, however, we have passed a great divide and our period of extensive growth has come gradually to an end. The agricultural frontier closed in two phases. The first transition came in the 1890s and the second during the 1920s. In the development of our mineral resources, we have seen a similar transformation. Through the 1930s, Americans continued to bring into production heretofore unknown supplies of gas and oil; the Gulf Coast finds were followed by the exploitation of the even more spectacular East Texas fields. Since that time, however, domestic discoveries have been less impressive and the cost of development higher. These two characteristics apply to the offshore discoveries and to the Alaskan fields as well. The future is described in negative terms by even the most optimistic observers, all of whom agree that major oil finds of the sort that characterized the past are unlikely to be made in the years ahead.

Pronouncements such as these evoke considerable gloom of late, but what, after all, would one expect after more than a century of active exploration for domestic oil? Similar predictions can and have been advanced about America's coal supplies, copper, and iron ore, all of which in the past have been focal points for the same type of exploitation that took place in oil, agriculture, and timber. Insofar as major natural resources are concerned, America has crossed the divide that separates a young developing nation with seemingly unlimited sources of supply from a middle-aged country whose resources are well charted, clearly finite, and deserving of conservation as well as exploitation.

It is hardly any accident that the conservation movement is primarily a twentieth-century phenomenon in the United States. Through most of our history, conservation was unnecessary. We had too many natural resources to waste time worrying about conserving them. In the present century, however, we have become concerned about our soil, our timber, our oil and water, about all of our resources—and with good cause. Rapid extensive development of the sort that wastes resources has in this century become less and less acceptable to more and more Americans for reasons that make economic as well as political sense. Local governments have opted for planned development, states have sought to clean up their rivers and lakes, and agencies of the federal government have tried to protect our land, water, and air. The middle-aged nation learns to husband its resources or it learns to do without them.

The balance between resources, capital, and labor has shifted decisively. The United States has become a capital-rich economy (relative, that is, to its resources). During our three centuries of extensive growth, we imported capital from abroad. In this century, however, we have become a creditor nation that sends vast amounts of capital overseas to take advantage of economic opportunities in other countries. In the twentieth century we have also gradually become a labor-rich society (again, relative to our resources and the opportunities they create). As America crossed this divide, our days of slam-bang, extensive growth were left behind. In our new economic setting expansion was achieved primarily through increases in efficiency. Advances in productivity became as crucial to our continued success as new resources once were. Technological and organizational innovations assumed a central role in our economic life. Ours was now an intensive economy.

This new style of mature economy grew more slowly, and Americans understandably became more concerned in this century about their economic security. To achieve a greater measure of protection they developed a host of new public and private institutions. Many of these are familiar to you. Our elaborate social welfare system comes to mind immediately, as do such organizations as industrial unions and farm co-operatives. Others—including, for example, our professional associations—may be less familiar. In the following chapters we will look more carefully at these organizations and at the ways they protect their members' interests. Some of these new economic institutions—our giant industrial corporations, for instance—make us uneasy at times. Periodically we long to return to the old days of unrestrained expansion and individual effort. But that of course is impossible, in part because few of us want to sacrifice the measure of security the new institutional setting has provided us.

Still, when we see how substantial the changes have been in our economic life, it is easy to understand why so many Americans have been upset in recent years. Even when the new system has performed very well—and on balance it has been successful in meeting our needs for both security and growth—it has provoked criticism simply because it is so different from the system that we associate with our nation's youth. When the new institutions perform poorly, as has been the case in the last few years, we are doubly critical. Then we are angry about the nature of these strange organizations and also about their performance. Then we feel an especially intense longing to recapture our past glory, to cross back over the great divide between youth and middle age, between the extensive and the intensive economy.

V

These three major watersheds—in geography, demography, and economy—stand out clearly when we look back over our history from the perspective of the 1980s. For Americans who lived through these developments, however, it was difficult to see that such decisive changes were taking place. They experienced all of them as a series of discrete problems; like us today, they were just trying to stay in the correct lane and get across the bridge. They dealt with one difficulty at a time, usually by tinkering with our society's institutions. America's public or private organizations (sometimes both) were thus altered to solve this or that problem, to remove this or that obstacle to our progress.

Gradually over the decades since 1900 these incremental changes accumulated and have now reached a formidable total. We have, it seems, erected a largely new and very durable institutional structure suited to the conditions of middle age. This structure functions according to new principles. It serves us and our society in novel ways. In the next chapter we will look more closely at how some of these institutions evolved and at how they changed the United States.

3

THE NEW ECONOMIC INSTITUTIONS OF A MIDDLE-AGED SOCIETY, 1870–1940

History has been harsh to President Calvin Coolidge, but when you look at a picture of the man, you can understand why. There he stands, a dried up little fellow in a stiff white collar. Prim. Cautious. Laconic. Who would want to spend Friday evening drinking with Calvin Coolidge? If he came to your house for dinner, you would certainly stick him between two people who were more interesting conversationalists. That is what the picture and our historians tell us.

But as usual, historians are hanging judges (far more demanding of past leaders than they are of their current heroes). Coolidge was, after all, a very successful politician. In a decade remembered for frolics with gin and jazz, the people of the United States elected him to the nation's highest political post. He had to be more effective than those pictures and the funny stories make him seem, and indeed one of his talents was for pithy remarks that properly caught the temper of the times.

This was the case when he said, "The business of America is business." This aphorism could be understood in a narrow sense as a statement typical of a conservative, probusiness president speaking in a conservative, probusiness era. But actually Coolidge's remark had a broader significance insofar as it captured the mood of a society in which a variety of new economic institutions, all of which espoused "business methods," a "businesslike" approach to their affairs, were coming to prominence. These institutions had all developed in the years spanned by Coolidge's lifetime. The business methods of the twenties were new. The leading institutions of that decade—whether they served businessmen, laborers, professionals, or farmers—were those associated with the historical watershed that interests us, with the transition to an intensive, a more mature economy. We need to understand what it was that they meant by "business methods."

II

In agriculture these new and powerful institutions had all evolved in the years since Coolidge was born in Vermont in 1872. At that time the family farm had been the basic producing unit in agriculture. Then the entire agricultural system was still expanding, reaching out to as yet unexploited land. Vermont was far from this agricultural frontier, of course, and New England farmers were not reaping the benefits of growth. To the west, however, there was still fertile land to be settled— land that promised to yield substantial profits from commercial agriculture and from capital gains if the farmer or his sons eventually sold the land and moved on.

One year later, however, a disastrous panic and a long depression interrupted the process of economic betterment in agriculture and in other parts of the economy as well. In the years that followed, farmers throughout the nation began to look for new ideas and new types of organizations that would enable them to protect their incomes and capital gains from downturns of this sort. They did not suddenly lose their interest in new economic opportunities; they just began to give more thought to security. At first they were rather hesitant about this. Like a young father buying insurance for the first time, they were uncertain how safe they wanted to be. When prices improved, even temporarily, they were inclined to forget about long-run security and think about short-run profits. But then when prices dipped lower, they would again take up the quest. In the 1880s and 1890s, they tried and abandoned a number of ideas that seemed initially to promise a solution to their difficulties.

The central problem for the farmer was to find a way to achieve control of production and thus prices of farm commodities. From our perspective today that seems obvious. But to many farmers in the late nineteenth century other problems loomed very large. For a time, the farmer's organizations were beguiled by the money problem (should the U.S. stay on the gold standard?), distracted by the question of railroad regulation, and periodically agitated over the need to break up monopolies in manufacturing and commerce. To some it appeared that the best way to solve the farmer's problems was to establish cooperatives that would enable their members to lower the prices of the things they bought or increase the prices of the things they sold or both. Others promoted the idea that adopting better methods of farming would improve conditions.

Not until the early 1900s did farm leaders and their organizations begin to forge a significant measure of agreement that the central problem involved production and prices. Then it took more decades and numerous additional forays into peripheral economic issues before the consensus about controlling production and prices was strong enough to enable farmers to push through Congress legislation aimed at solving this central problem. The consensus was engineered by a new type of agricultural organization—typified by the Farm Bureau Federation—that avoided radicalism and strong rhetoric. The bureau and similar organizations such as the American Wheat Growers, Associated, did not want to get rid of monopolies;

they wanted to imitate them. They wanted the farmer to have the same sort of economic power that U.S. Steel and Standard Oil had. That was what they meant by business methods. But in the case of agriculture, that power could be achieved only with government support. They sought that power by operating just as other interest groups did, pressing Congress to help them use public power to solve the farmers' private economic problems.

The first fruits of this effort ripened and fell off the tree in the 1920s. The farm organizations and their friendly congressmen pushed through a measure that authorized agricultural cooperatives to control prices in much the same way that the Organization of Petroleum Exporting Countries, OPEC, is currently manipulating the price of oil. But there were too many farms and too many farmers to control in this way. A stronger system was needed, and Congress tried to provide this in 1927 when it passed the McNary-Haugen Bill. But Calvin Coolidge promptly condemned and vetoed this measure. The government, Coolidge said, had no business supporting the prices of particular agricultural commodities by helping farmers get rid of their surpluses. He made the veto stick that year and also in 1928 when the farm groups drove a modified form of the bill through Congress again. The business of America was not, Coolidge said, price-fixing.

The farm organizations and their members disagreed. They mounted even more pressure on the government to introduce a public-private system of controls that would protect the farmer's income and status. In 1929 they got about one-tenth of the loaf they wanted when Herbert Hoover signed the Agricultural Marketing Act, which established a new Federal Farm Board. The board set out to help farm groups deal with their surpluses, but the Great Depression of the 1930s soon buried the board's program just as it did Herbert Hoover's political career and reputation.

After Franklin D. Roosevelt took office in 1933, the

farmers got the rest of the loaf. The New Deal's agricultural policies provoked substantial controversy, in part because they sought to bolster prices by cutting production at a time when many Americans were unable to afford the food they needed. But in this regard the farm policies of the thirties were no different from those implemented on behalf of several other economic groups. All aimed to master the market, to employ controls that would provide social and economic security over the long run. By the end of the decade the farmers producing the major commodities in this country had these sorts of controls and were sheltered from the fiercest winds of economic change. They had thus completed one significant part of their institutional adjustment to America's economic maturity.

By that date farmers could also point with some pride to a new set of public-private institutions dedicated to improving productivity in agriculture. During those same decades when farmers were groping for the means to control prices and production, they were also gradually building up federal and state organizations designed to perform two other tasks essential to an intensive economy. The first job was that of generating new ideas. Ideas about crops, about farming techniques, about breeding animals. Ideas grounded in the chemistry of the soil, the biology of insect and animal life, the mechanics of harvesting methods. The second job was to distribute this information by helping real dirt farmers implement the ideas.

Here were two tasks that even Coolidge thought the government should help perform. Over his lifetime the United States had developed an elaborate system of organizations to do these two jobs. While the federal government and especially the Department of Agriculture had a central position in that system, many other public and private organizations were involved. State universities and experimental stations helped. So did the farmers' own associations and private foundations.

Farm newspapers and magazines contributed. By the end of the 1930s this entire system was very big, unbelievably complex, but still not very successful.

What was the problem? The first task, that of developing new ideas, was being done very well. In most areas of agricultural research, the United States was by that time the leading country in the world. The problem was that U.S. farmers were very slow to accept these new concepts, slow to change traditional methods of farming, suspicious of what they called book farmers. As a result, productivity—the crucial measure of efficiency—was increasing at a slow rate. From the beginning of the century through the end of the First World War, in fact, productivity in agriculture actually declined.

All that was needed, however, was the kind of patience that Coolidge personified and that most of us find so hard to muster. Instead of abandoning the new system, the United States continued to support it, building up a great backlog of new ideas and working closely with the farmers who would have to apply them. In the twenties and thirties they started to do just that, and finally in the 1940s America began to experience revolutionary advances in agricultural productivity. By that time the nation's farmers had good cause to be satisfied with the new types of economic institutions they had developed in this century. Both sets of institutions were important to them: the production controls and price supports protected their current income and wealth; the organizations promoting increased productivity were the key to the future, to growth in the intensive economy of the twentieth century.

III

Executives in the nation's major businesses at that time were as interested as farmers in these two goals. They too had developed entirely new sorts of organizations to achieve these same objectives. While the new business organizations made far less use of government power than the farm groups did, businessmen were flexible about means as long as they worked. Where private solutions had failed and public programs had been needed (as they were, for example, in the oil industry), business had not hesitated to harness state and federal power to the engine of capitalism.

The primary institutional innovations in business, however, were those in the private sector and chief among these was the modern corporation. As late as 1880, when the United States was already one of the world's leading industrial powers, only a few such corporations existed in this country and they were all in transportation. In this regard, the railroads ran at least twenty years ahead of the rest of the business system. By 1900, however, manufacturing was catching up, as a wave of mergers transformed American industry. In some instances, giant corporations emerged as a result of vertical integration* and growth founded upon highly efficient modes of production and distribution. The leading meat packers developed in this manner, as did the dominant producers of electrical machinery. In more cases, however, great combines were created initially by horizontal integration which brought together under one corporate roof most of the companies competing in one phase of an industry—for example, refining in the oil industry, the core of John D. Rockefeller's great corporate empire.

Whatever the path to combination, one of the results was to concentrate production in the hands of a few companies. These giant corporations learned how to protect their positions in the economy by avoiding intense price competition. At first, businessmen thought they might have to control an entire industry to achieve this goal. Hence Rockefeller's drive to monopolize the entire oil industry, a drive that was at one time ninety percent successful. But as Standard Oil's executives

*Vertical integration brings together in one company the heretofore separate units engaged in producing raw materials, in transporting them, manufacturing the goods, and then distributing the final products.

learned, they could protect their interests from the immediate pressures of the marketplace so long as most of the industry's production was controlled by a few such large firms. Normally there were a number of smaller competitors—the so-called "tail" of the industry—clustered around the great combines. Over the long run, the performance of the smaller businesses proved to be important to the industry—and especially important to consumers. But in the short run, all of these industries were dominated by the decisions made by the largest competitors, who between themselves usually controlled from half to ninety percent of the industry's productive capacity.

The great corporations used their power to stabilize prices, market shares, and hence profits. Like the farmers, they had to learn how to do this. In the years following the first great wave of mergers at the turn of the century, many of these oligopolistic industries* suffered from periodic outbreaks of rough-and-tumble competition of the old, nineteenth-century style. Some of the largest firms went under. But by the end of the First World War, the managers of most of the country's great corporations had learned that they were all likely to suffer when they competed without restraint. It was better, they discovered, to share the market than to contest it through price competition. After 1920 hardly any of our largest companies went out of business. They had, it seems, conquered death: by curing the disease of price competition, they had virtually eliminated bankruptcy (for themselves, that is!). This part of their transition to the modern economy was finished in most industries by 1920, and so successful were these firms that they were more than able to hold their own during the

---

*An "oligopoly" is an industry in which a few producers (the Greek word *oligos* means "few") control most of the output. These companies are also frequently referred to as "center firms" because of their central position in their respective industries and in the national economy. I have not used that expression, however, because several of my students have confessed to me that they always think about girdle advertisements when I mention a "center firm."

Great Depression. The country's largest industrial corporations successfully weathered the worst years of the thirties and most were able to make some profits even when the national economy was running at half speed.

For those industries that were unable to bring their markets under control, the search for security frequently resulted in some form of public-private institution of the sort that farmers had finally developed. In banking the Federal Reserve System helped to meet these needs for many of the nation's leading financial institutions, as did the Federal Deposit Insurance Corporation. In oil, where production in the southwestern fields produced chaotic conditions in the twenties and thirties, a curious amalgam of state and federal regulation emerged in the 1930s to balance production with demand and stabilize price levels. In other industries firms learned to manipulate regulatory systems—even those that had been imposed on the businesses by reformers. The regulated firms "captured" the regulatory agencies and used them to control entry and to stabilize prices at profitable levels. Shipping firms did this with the U.S. Maritime Commission, an independent regulatory commission which in effect fixed prices on behalf of the companies it was supposed to be regulating. The agencies in charge of many other industries performed in a similar manner. Whatever the particular form these arrangements took, they all had the same result: the businesses in the industry were protected, their income and status made more secure by the new systems of control.

In addition to such controls, however, businessmen in the modern, intensive economy needed new ideas and new institutions to implement them (just as farmers did). Businessmen too sought to improve the efficiency of their operations, to develop novel products and methods of production. The first step in this direction normally came very soon after one of the great combines had been formed. The corporation's leaders then had to bring their widespread holdings under tighter control. Administrative consolidation was the key to efficiency at this stage in the firm's development. Usually the company's accounting techniques had to be improved. Then the firm's managers could compare various operations and concentrate production in their most efficient plants. They had to devise new methods of organizing the work force. The profits to be reaped from internal innovations such as these were very great in most cases, and once implemented, the new programs gave these corporate giants even greater protection than they already had from existing or potential competitors.

To ensure that the firm also had an adequate supply of new ideas over the long haul, a few of the largest companies began even before World War I to set up their own research laboratories. The leaders were in the technologically advanced, science-based industries, and by 1920, these corporations were employing highly skilled scientists and engineers to do both basic and applied research. They were investing large amounts of money in their research and development (R & D) programs, and the results were impressive, both to the general public and to other businesses—including their competitors.

In the 1920s R & D became extremely popular among American businesses. By that time, most of the nation's largest firms had consolidated their market positions and improved their internal administrative controls. They had wartime profits to spend, and they put more and more of their capital into research. The results showed in the national figures on productivity growth. During the two decades before the First World War, productivity in industry had increased, but the rate of growth had not been very impressive. In the 1920s and 1930s, by contrast, American businesses were extremely successful in improving their efficiency. By that time, the country's corporate giants had made a successful transition to the twentieth-century economy. They were insulated from short-term market pressures. They had also learned how to improve their internal efficiency and to achieve the growth that would protect their financial positions over the long run.

IV

In the late 1930s, laborers who worked for these great firms had less reason to feel secure than their bosses, but labor too had developed a remarkable number of new organizations to protect its interests. Strongest and oldest of these were the national unions of skilled craftsmen, many of which dated from the nineteenth century. They had brought together for collective action the men and sometimes the women in a number of the building, service, and manufacturing trades. These organized laborers were at first a tiny elite in the work force. Their unions were weak, their bargaining power sharply limited. The early labor organizations, like the farm groups, frequently got tangled up with reform issues that had at best a slim relationship to the workers' central problem. For workers the crucial issue was to find the means of gaining power over the work place. They needed this power so they could exert some control over their incomes, their work conditions, and their security on the job.

Near the end of the century, after the several national unions had formed a federation, the labor movement began to focus on this central issue. Its ideology was given pithy expression by Samuel Gompers, who headed the American Federation of Labor (AFL). Asked what labor wanted, Gompers replied: "More, More, More." By the early 1900s, his outlook and the craft unions making up the AFL dominated the labor movement in America.

To these unions the rise of corporate combines and the new emphasis these companies placed on productivity gains posed clear threats. The modern corporations had financial resources that dwarfed those of the unions. These companies were normally in the most technologically advanced sectors of the economy, and there the traditional skills either had been supplanted or were threatened by new and more efficient methods of production. In the steel industry, for instance, J. P. Morgan's great combine, the U.S. Steel Corporation, was able in the early 1900s to break the back of one of the country's strongest craft unions.

The trade organizations responded to technological change in a creative, although not entirely successful, fashion. Where new methods of producing metal parts made the skilled machinist obsolete, the unions simply labeled the new jobs in the old way. If master carpenters were no longer in demand, then the Carpenters Union would ooze out, amoebalike, to absorb the new low-skill occupations. In this way, the labor movement centered around the AFL continued to gain power over jobs, incomes, and work conditions in the years before 1920. By the end of World War I, in fact, there were over four million workers in labor unions in the United States, most of them in AFL organizations.

Still, the unions were having trouble in the most advanced sectors of the economy. They were unable to regain the position they had lost in iron and steel, unable to organize the rapidly growing automobile industry. Even in 1920, when membership in trade groups was at its peak, less than twenty percent of the work force was organized. In the next decade this situation worsened. The quickening pace of technological change created new problems for organized labor, as did the mood of a country which clearly did not think the major enterprise of America was celebrated on Labor Day. The Republican administrations of the twenties accurately reflected that mood. After all, Calvin Coolidge had come to national prominence by breaking the policemen's strike in Boston in 1919.

Labor was thus not tempted in these years to emulate the organized farmers who were turning to the federal government for support. Actually, at no time from the late nineteenth century through the early 1930s did the nation's trade unions seek the power they needed in the public sector. Labor was suspicious of government officials, who seemed too cozy with the employers, and the unions sought to control their markets by dealing directly with their business adversaries. During the years of progressive reform (roughly 1900 to 1919), state and federal governments passed a number of labor laws designed to regulate particular aspects of the working conditions of particular groups (including, for instance, working conditions for women and children); during the First World War, too, labor played a significant role in the wartime economic agencies. But on balance labor looked to private, not public power for the solution to its central problem.

In the Great Depression of the 1930s, however, U.S. labor rudely reversed its course of action. From 1932 on, organized labor was deeply involved with public policy, and the new institutional structure that labor built in the years that followed gave to the government a substantial—often a controlling—role in labor-management relations. The primary building blocks of this new public-private structure were still national unions; many were craft unions but many others were the new type of industrial union that evolved after 1934. Above these stood two federations—the AFL and a new Congress of Industrial Organizations (CIO). But above these now stood a National Labor Relations Board, which was empowered to make decisions vital to organized labor and to its employers. While the quality of these decisions has been extensively debated, one aspect of the NLRB's short history seems beyond controversy: the board used federal power in a way that enabled the unions, new and old, to solve their central problem—that is, to achieve a significant measure of power over the markets in which their members sold their labor.

By 1940 this new system was securely in place. The unions had penetrated the mass-production industries. There were 3.6 million men and women in the new industrial unions of the CIO and 4.2 million in trade unions affiliated with the

AFL. Union members on the eve of World War II made up twenty-seven percent of the work force (nonfarm) in the United States. In many of the nation's most important industries, the workers' organizations had acquired the power they needed to enforce seniority rules and to protect their members from arbitrary dismissal; they could also exercise a substantial measure of influence over their members' incomes and work conditions. They could do nothing about the high rate of unemployment that still existed in 1940, but they could provide for organized labor the same types of controls that farmers and businessmen had introduced in their spheres of the economy.

V

There were other sorts of laborers who charted a different course toward this same home port. They were the middle-class professionals whose numbers have grown so rapidly in our highly organized, intensive economy. They too used a special blend of public and private power to achieve their goals, but in their case, the public authority was normally at the state or local level. There, for instance, they were frequently able to control entry to the profession by establishing some form of licensing law which could be used to prevent too many new competitors from going into practice. Another means of achieving the same end was to set very high educational standards for the profession or to limit sharply the number of positions in the professional schools (as was the case with doctors, who were among the most successful in choking off entry). Measures such as these enabled professionals to protect their incomes and jobs, although of course the controls adopted usually were not discussed publicly in these terms.

The public discourse was framed along lines stressing the need to provide consumers with protection from the inferior services that would be provided by poorly trained practitioners. Before the members of a profession could convince a state or local government that this was the case, however, they first had to build up their own private organizations. These institutions have enjoyed a remarkable growth in the past century. When Coolidge was a young boy, only a few professions were organized in America. There were doctors, lawyers, and engineers, groups which had each created a variety of local, state, and national associations. These professions had gained widespread acceptance, and the public seems to have conceded that their practices involved an essential mystery, a special body of knowledge that the layman could not be expected to master on his own. Hence the public's willingness to accept the idea that entry had to be limited. This also accounts for the fact that the professionals themselves were so often given a leading role, and sometimes the only role, in determining who was qualified to be a member of the profession.

The demand for such controls increased sharply in the latter part of the nineteenth century as many new professions emerged and old ones broke into specialized subprofessions. By 1900 America was abuzz with professional activity. New organizations were springing up in the major cities at an astonishing rate, each one proclaiming the need for public recognition of its special status and its members' special needs. In some cases these needs did not include control of entry. Frequently they did. At times a profession failed to get what it asked for; this was the case, for instance, with the doctors who tried with only partial success to use public power to impose restraints on osteopaths. The leaders of the mainline medical organizations looked on osteopathy as quackery. By bringing the osteopaths under the direct control of the state boards of medical examiners, they hoped to curtail, or perhaps eliminate, this form of competition. They would—as they saw it—also raise the standards of medical practice in the states involved. What a pleasant combination of private and public welfare! But alas, most states disagreed and denied the medical associations the complete victory they sought. After all, the doctors' organizations already had control of their own profession. While they did not have all the power they sought, by the 1920s they had successfully cultivated a thick, protective hedge of regulations and commissions. State power gave the doctors and many other professionals a good measure of control over entry, the standards of the practice, and thus the terms of competition.

Baltimore, Maryland—my home city—was typical of the American scene. By 1920 there were at least thirty professional organizations that had offices and were active in Baltimore. These included the bar association, the city medical society, their opponents in the Maryland Osteopathic Association, several nurses' organizations, the National Association of Stationary Engineers, the organizations of the military engineers, bay pilots, life and fire underwriters, druggists, teachers, dentists, veterinarians, certified public accountants, and more. All worked through the city and state governments to protect their members' immediate interests and promote the advancement of the profession.

By that time a number of these professions had achieved a substantial measure of control over who entered practice, what type of education the practitioner needed, and how that person should behave in order to preserve good standing among his or her peers. Attorneys had enjoyed this sort of power for many years, as had such health-related professionals as doctors, pharmacists, nurses, and dentists. Dentistry was typical of the lot. To practice in Maryland a dentist had to have a certificate from the state board of dental examiners. The board was made up of six practicing dentists, selected from a list presented to the governor by the state dental association. It was thus very important to have an effective organization representing the profession. The association and its chosen representatives played a vital role in this sort of public-private system of controls.

As might have been expected, this sort of power attracted newcomers, some of whom had slightly questionable professional credentials. There was no reason to doubt the public interest in and respect for the special knowledge (the mystery) of the bay pilots who brought ships into Baltimore, or the certified public accountants, the optometrists, the foot doctors, the veterinarians, or the stationary engineers (who were skilled in running steam engines and boilers)—all of whom had arrangements similar to those of the doctors and dentists. But now this sort of sheltering umbrella was also handed to barbers, to plumbers, to undertakers, to osteopaths, and, yes, even to chiropractors. The list continued to grow. In the hard times of the thirties, architects and all professional engineers won the right to determine who their competitors would be, and so too did hairdressers, beauty culturists (including manicurists, a calling whose claim to professional status you may have some difficulty understanding), and land surveyors. Even real estate brokers were served by a state commission with authority to issue licenses, but as yet the commission did not give an examination or specify educational requirements. It did, nevertheless, attempt to curtail such threatening practices as fee splitting, which was often a way of cutting prices to consumers.

During the Great Depression, the threat of competition (that is, the threat to the income of the professionals themselves) was particularly acute. The dentists in Maryland responded by raising the ethical standards of their calling; in 1937 they prohibited virtually all advertising. No dentist could thereafter advertise his prices, his superior skills, or the painlessness with which he repaired your mouth. The four-square professional dentist would instead place discreet signs—no more than two—on his place of business and letters in those signs would "not exceed three inches square." At about the same time the pharmacists strengthened their positions by using the law to beat back competitors who were cutting into their trade with prepackaged drugs and other materials. The undertakers used the state's authority to fend off the corporations that were opening branch funeral parlors in the state.

Maryland was not exceptional. Next week if you drive your kids to the library, don't wait in the car. Go in with them and look at a copy of your state's laws as of 1940. What you will find is a labyrinth of similar regulations. In state after state, the markets for professional services were by 1940 dense with controls, most of which were designed to protect the professionals themselves from what they thought was unreasonable competition. During the hard times of the thirties, almost any competition seemed unreasonable to many of the nation's professionals, and they used their systems of controls and professional groups in an effort to shore up their sagging economic positions.

Paradoxically, these same institutions were the ones that the same professionals used to ensure that their calling would continue to generate and implement new ideas. In an intensive economy, as we have seen, this sort of continuing innovation was as essential to the nation as it was to the individual or organization. All of the main-line, successful professions recognized this need and took steps early on to ensure that the body of knowledge that constituted the group's central mystery would continue to grow—forever.

What sorts of measures were these? In a pivotal role were the state educational institutions which trained preprofessionals and got them ready for their exams. The teachers in these schools were also crucial agents in generating new ideas for the profession. It was important to have your own department or school in which tenured professors (who themselves were happily sheltered from competition) could endlessly turn out academic articles and books, could manage research teams, and could direct the Ph.D. candidates who would man the system in the next generation.* Publications serving the professions and regular conventions (whose proceedings could also be published) helped to spread the ideas, as did private businesses which in some cases profited from the sales of goods handled by the practitioners. Every bona fide profession developed these types of institutions. Along with them went a set of values that stressed progress (as defined by the profession itself). We are most familiar with this in the scientific professions, where priority of innovation may make the difference between a Nobel Prize winner and a drone. But all of the established professions—and some that were not very well established—embraced similar values and supported professional organizations which sought to ensure that such progress was actually achieved.

Most of these institutions had been created since the late nineteenth century. They had, in toto, significantly changed the quality of America's medical services, the nature of the goods people used, the type of education they received, the roads they drove over, the very buildings in which they worked. By 1940 the modern professions had achieved secure positions for themselves, while vigorously promoting the types of improvements in products and services that had become crucial to the growth of our economy and the improvement of our living conditions.

VI

Now we can see what was meant by "business methods" in the 1920s. Businessmen, farmers, laborers, and professionals were all developing new institutions which had certain goals in common. They all sought to provide their owners or members an increased measure of protection, of security, in the

*I am a full professor; I have tenure; and day after day, I happily put my shoulder to the wheel within a wheel that I am describing. Don't we all?

slower-growing economy of the twentieth century. They all achieved this goal by acquiring and exercising power in the appropriate marketplace. Sometimes the power was private. Sometimes public. Most often it was a combination of the two, with the balance shaded toward the private side.

These institutions—whether they were run on behalf of dentists or farmers or manufacturers or the men who worked for them—all represented a basically realistic accommodation to the major changes that were taking place in America's geography, demography, and economy. If the new organizations stressed orderly patterns of development, if they gave somewhat more attention to the bird in hand than the ones in the bush, their perceptions of our society were entirely accurate. The United States had changed, had left behind its long phase of rapid growth. As individuals, Americans were buying more and more insurance. As a society, they had introduced in the thirties a new national system of social security. What could be more appropriate than new institutions that could help various groups of our citizens steer a prudent, businesslike course into middle age?

It was equally appropriate that most of these institutions also stressed the need to develop and introduce new ideas that made for greater efficiency. Innovation was the key to growth and continued success in America's modern economy. Business methods also involved new and (one always hoped) more effective ways of doing things. Science and system were to be harnessed. They would pull the country ahead even though the old frontiers were gone.

From the vantage point of 1940, however, it was as yet unclear that this new economic system would be as successful as the one it had replaced. During the previous twenty years, the United States' record had been mixed and confusing. In the twenties America had achieved substantial increases in productivity. New products and entirely new industries had characterized this decade of prosperity. Not all Americans shared equally in the good times (many farmers, for instance, were having serious problems then), but there was reason to believe in the twenties that the new business methods were working and that intensive growth would keep the nation moving ahead.

The Great Depression cast a dark shadow on that conclusion. By 1933 the country's Gross National Product had been cut by almost fifty percent. While productivity continued to increase during the depression, it was difficult to take much pleasure in that record when seventeen million were unemployed. With the nation's banking system weakened and, for a time, closed down, with state and local governments unable to meet their obligations either to their citizens or their lenders, the United States began to look for entirely new ways to bring its economy under control. Seven years later, in 1940, after substantial experimentation with various types of federal programs ranging from traditional modes of regulation and subsidy to more novel experiments in regional (TVA) and industry-wide (NRA) planning, the United States was still struggling to get back to the level of national income that had been achieved in the late twenties. There were still millions unemployed. The experience with the depression and New Deal strongly suggested that the United States might have far less aptitude for intensive economic development than it had displayed for the chaotic style of extensive growth that had prevailed in previous centuries.

What a cruel joke this seemed to play on the groups served by the new economic institutions. They had successfully carved out relatively secure positions for themselves. But now it appeared that they might be forced to struggle just to hang on to their piece of a shrunken economic pie. None of the leaders of these organizations had given much thought to how the entire economy might be controlled. During the thirties they had frequently expressed opinions about individual New Deal programs, but their concept of their responsibilities was particular to their group. They had been no better prepared than the country's political leaders to guide the country out of the valley of the Great Depression. They had been unable to provide effective leadership as the government floundered about, looking for some means of spurring a general recovery.

In 1940 it looked as if that goal might never be achieved. In fact, given the record of the last few years of depression, there was cause to be concerned that the pie might actually shrink again. Even the leaders of some of the country's largest corporations were nervous about that possibility. They were eager to find some means of controlling the level of economic activity in the entire United States economy. They were ready to concede that this would have to be done by the federal government. But as late as 1940, it was not at all clear exactly how that could be done.

4

FROM DEMOCRACY TO
TRIOCRACY, 1870–1940

If you had visited Washington, D.C., in 1940, you quickly could have learned why it was so difficult for our government to establish a program that would effectively control the level of economic activity in the United States. A day spent in Congress, in one of the agencies, or in a department such as Agriculture would have been very instructive. At the Department of Agriculture's great limestone labyrinth on the corner of Independence Avenue and 14th Street you could have chatted with some of the thousands of government employees who toiled there on behalf of America's farms and farmers. If you talked to enough of these agrarian bureaucrats, you would probably have noticed that they were not peas in a pod, all alike in outlook, in appearance, in interests. In fact, there were two distinct classes of employees at Agriculture. One group talked the language of Washington, the language of power and profession. These workers were attentive to the terms of trade for American commodities being sold abroad; they were the sort who wrote and read the U.S.D.A. technical bulletins. They were interested in markets and in the *Farm Credit Quarterly*. They were Washington-centered—tuned in to the concerns and endless ripples of political small talk that moved across the surface of life in the capital. The other group looked and sounded and acted in a different way. Many of them drawled a bit, sounding like those folks out on the farm to whom they regularly sent instructions on "Soybeans: Culture and Varieties" or on getting the most out of fertilizer. This group of bureaucrats could get excited about erosion and about the prospects of saving soil moisture by contour tillage.

These two groups of officials accurately reflected the major interests of the department. Agriculture had one face turned toward Washington and especially toward Congress, which voted the department its funds, determined the scope of its programs, and approved the appointments of its top officials. Potomac politics was very much on the minds of these bureaucrats, from Secretary of Agriculture Claude R. Wickard down to the clerks in the Bureau of Agricultural Economics. The other face of the department was turned toward its clients, who raised cotton in Texas, corn in Iowa, and wheat in Montana. Sometimes these farmers raised hell in Washington when they didn't get their way. When that happened, their feelings were soothed by those department representatives who talked like Johnny Cash, understood dirt farming, and were always sympathetic about the problems of agriculture.

Neither group, however, had a direct, primary interest in what happened to the entire U.S. economy. In that regard they closely resembled the rest of the almost one million persons working for the federal government in 1940. Just about all of these employees had very specific responsibilities to serve very specific groups. Whether they helped businessmen or veterans or laborers or farmers, whether they were primarily interested in credit systems, in the Panama Canal, in consular services, or in the U.S. Navy, they had their eyes fixed either on their clients or on Congress. That left the national economy as an appropriate subject for lunchtime discussions, but not for federal action. To the contrary, departments such as Agriculture had every reason to see all national economic problems through lenses colored by the immediate concerns of one part of the population, in this case that twenty-one percent of the American work force that was still actively engaged in farming.

Of course farmers themselves did not spend much time in Washington making their feelings known to the Department of Agriculture. You could have spent all day in the department's south building without meeting one person with manure on his shoes. You might, however, have bumped into a spokesman from one of the numerous agrarian organizations. They were the ones who protected the farmer's interests in the nation's capital. In 1940 the Farm Bureau was one of the most powerful of these interest groups, and when Ed O'Neal of the bureau dropped in at the corner of Independence and 14th, he was certain to receive a cordial reception. So close were the relationships between the bureau and the department during these years that the Farm Bureau could with justice take credit for most of the major acts of legislation that recast America's farm policies in the thirties.

Working together, the representatives of organizations such as the bureau and the department's officials could swing considerable weight in Congress. For years the farm bloc—consisting of representatives and senators from states where agriculture was a major occupation—had been maneuvering legislation favored by the farm groups through Congress. While some of these measures had been vetoed during the 1920s, most of them had passed and been signed into law in the thirties. Indeed, by 1940 the ties between Congress, the farm organizations, and the Department of Agriculture were very close, durable, and mutually productive. The department was able to protect its budget, its prerogatives, and its major programs from all but the most determined and widespread opposition. The farm interest groups could deliver to their

members legislation that supported those long-standing programs aimed at improving agricultural productivity as well
as the newer ones dedicated to protecting the farmer's income
and status. The congressmen and senators could, for their
part, look forward to a long career on Capitol Hill so long
as this tripartite alliance could produce favorable results for
their country constituents.

The political links between the department, the interest
groups, and the Congress were far more important than the
department's ties with the president, even with an unusually
forceful president like Franklin D. Roosevelt. FDR had personally approved the appointment of Secretary of Agriculture
Claude R. Wickard, and of his predecessor Henry A. Wallace.
But even those decisions had been shaped for Roosevelt by
the aggressive farm lobbyists, by powerful congressmen in
the Democratic party, and by spokesmen from the department.
This strong three-sided alliance had screened FDR's choices,
preshaping appointments just as it did policy decisions involving
agriculture. After all, in 1940 (or any other year) the president
could only give an hour here and an hour there to thinking
about agriculture. The central figures in agriculture's triple
alliance thought about little else.

The congressional/interest group/department combine
also had a far more dramatic influence upon public policy
than did the judiciary. This was true even during the thirties
when the Supreme Court struck down major parts of the
New Deal program for agriculture. In 1936 the Court ruled
that the Agricultural Adjustment Act (1933) was an uncon-
stitutional form of production control; in the previous year,
the Court had held that the Frazier-Lemke Amendment vi-
olated the Constitution in an effort to shield from bankruptcy
those farmers who had borrowed money and were unable to
pay their creditors. In both cases, however, Congress had
merely passed revised legislation that achieved the same ends.
Production control was renamed soil conservation, and that

satisfied the judiciary, just as it did the agrarian triple alliance which had led the drive for national controls in the first place.

Both the judiciary and the chief executive could exercise their greatest influence on policies such as these when they were first being promoted and implemented. Then they could sometimes block innovations (as Coolidge did when he vetoed the farm bills in 1927 and 1928), or actively promote them (as FDR did in 1933), or alter the precise form the policies took (as Herbert Hoover and the Supreme Court did on separate occasions during the thirties). It was dangerous, however, for any elected official from the president on down to reject completely the demands of such a powerful and well-organized combine as the one that served agriculture. Coolidge had succeeded. But a few years later the farmers got what they wanted anyway, and by that time Coolidge's party was sliding down into the minority position that it would continue to hold for decades to come.

Once programs such as those serving agriculture were securely in place, were achieving even modest success, and were running without generating major scandals, there was even less that the chief executive could do to change them. He might, perhaps, shift administrative control of a program, as Roosevelt did in 1939 when he took away the Farm Credit Administration's independent status and placed it under the direct control of the secretary of agriculture. He might, perhaps, force changes in the leadership of an agency or department. But each such tactical move could be politically expensive if it aroused strong interest-group opposition. If the interest groups allied themselves with Congress and with government officials in the agency or department involved, the president could well find his hands completely tied. That would be the most likely outcome if the president tried to alter significantly the operations or goals of a well-entrenched program. FDR avoided such conflicts, as have most of our modern presidents. As a result, by 1940 American government at all levels was pervaded by programs of this sort, programs securely anchored in alliances between the legislatures, the relevant interest groups, and department or agency bureaucrats. So formidable had these triple alliances become that they now were the central feature of our polity.

Democracy had thus given way in America to a new sort of political system that can best be called "Triocracy." In the triocratic government of 1940, the voters still had an important role to play. But their votes were now ancillary to the activities of the interest groups, the legislatures, and the bureaucrats who together shaped most of the country's most important public policies. These were the policies vital to the economic security and the progress of client groups such as those in agriculture and business. The voters could still decide whether they liked those policies. But neither the voters nor their political parties had as important a position in framing and sustaining public programs as they had held in the previous century. They had been supplanted by the country's triocracies. This form of government was the political counterpart to the new economic organizations described in the previous chapter. In polity as well as economy the United States had thus developed new and powerful institutions suited to the needs of a more mature society.

II

A glance back to the nineteenth century quickly tells us just how decisively the U.S. political system had changed. In the 1870s, when Calvin Coolidge was a young boy, the kind of political triumvirates that characterized our government in 1940 did not exist in their modern form. For one thing, there was, as yet, virtually no federal bureaucracy. The United States did not even have a civil service. There were about fifty thousand persons working for the federal government, only six thousand of them in Washington, D.C. None of them were shielded from swift and arbitrary dismissal by the party in power. The government worker who sought to bypass the party and its leadership, who sought through ties to client groups and Congress to build up an independent position— well, that person was likely very soon to be laboring in the private, not the public, sector.

Even at this early date, there was a Department of Agriculture, but it was as yet a mere seedling of the great bureaucracy that by the 1930s would sprawl over the southeast corner of the Mall. In the 1870s Agriculture did not have cabinet status. Commissioner of Agriculture Frederick Watts tried to promote the application of science to agriculture, but his efforts were severely restricted by the small size of his budget and staff. The entire department in 1875 had a budget of $233,780 and a staff of fifty-nine employees. All were tightly leashed to Congress, which specified in its annual budget provision the salaries and number of officials in each category: for example, one microscopist at $1,800; one assistant superintendent of the seed room at $1,200; one chief messenger at $840; and two assistant messengers at $720 each; and so on, through the entire department, from the commissioner down to the unskilled laborers (nine) who rounded out the list. In these circumstances the department toed the line, serving the immediate interests of the party in power. The Department of Agriculture was a mere governmental infant, incapable of independent action.

Even if the department had been more powerful, it could not have established alliances with the types of agricultural interest groups that were active in the 1930s. There was as yet no Farm Bureau, no Farmers Union, no National Cooperative Council. While the Patrons of Husbandry—known later as the Grange—was already in existence, that organization was struggling to avoid any involvement in politics. The modern agricultural interest groups would not take shape until some years later when American farmers began to perceive their problems in a new way and to look for new public policies that would shore up their economic position. The situation in agriculture was mirrored in other groups. There were particular organizations formed to achieve special objectives in the public realm. But most of these groups operated on a temporary, ad hoc basis. They could not form lasting alliances with government because they were themselves only temporary organizations. In the 1870s, then, two of the three types of institutions, the bureaucracies and the interest groups, that made up the triocracies of 1940 did not yet exist in their modern form.

In their absence, other institutions dominated the American democratic system. In the 1870s and the 1880s political parties had a central role to play in the governance of the United States. An overwhelming majority of those who were eligible to do so actually voted, and most of them had strong, enduring ties to one of the major parties. While the Democratic and Republican parties were both national in scope, much of their time was taken up with state and local issues such as prohibition (one of the foremost political questions in nineteenth-century America). These were the sorts of questions that elicited strong emotions and that welded your allegiance to the party of your choice (and often your father's choice as well—remember, mothers could not yet vote).

Identification with a particular party was in that setting an important determinant of status in the community. There were frequent occasions to march with, celebrate with, and be identified with fellow Democrats or Republicans. Even if you avoided these public displays of party loyalty, your political allegiance became general knowledge when you voted. The secret ballot had yet to be introduced in the United States. You went to vote carrying a distinctive ballot that normally had been supplied by one of the parties. Politics in that setting could involve individual questions of conscience, just as it does today, but political activity in the 1870s and 1880s had a far stronger social dimension than it does for most of us today.

Parties were relatively strong in the nineteenth century, as were the courts. Presidents had very little to preside over—the fifty-nine positions in the Department of Agriculture were typical of the small stakes. Congress too was less important than it would be in the twentieth century, if only because the legislature controlled far less wealth. Budgets were tiny in most circumstances. Congress could specify the wages of unskilled laborers and assistant messengers because it had so little else to do. Many of the questions facing the legislature were decided along party lines, and the Republicans and Democrats had formidable means of whipping their legislators into line. The courts were, by contrast, powerful agents of governance. They kept the presidents and Congress strictly accountable to the Constitution of the United States. Let the state government of Illinois seek to control railroad rates, and the U.S. Supreme Court would strike down the regulation as it did in 1886 (the Wabash case). Let the federal government establish in 1887 a new Interstate Commerce Commission to achieve a similar objective, and the federal courts would allow the ICC to exist but methodically strip it of its powers. Nor were the courts always just a negative force restraining change. They played a positive role in the nation's economic development, strengthening the hands of those entrepreneurs who were leading the drive to develop America's great resources. American democracy nineteenth-century style was an appropriate polity for a rich, aggressive nation experiencing rapid, extensive growth.

III

Not till the 1890s and the early decades of the twentieth century did this type of democratic system begin to give way in the United States. One important part of the transition was the development of our new economic institutions. Most of these organizations also functioned as political pressure groups, protecting their members' interests in local, state, and federal government. Since they normally operated on a permanent, ongoing basis, since they quickly developed professional staffs, since they often could muster a great deal of financial backing, these modern interest groups soon began to change decisively the American political landscape.

While they frequently worked through the political parties, the modern interest groups were less concerned with who was in office than they were with the achievement of their own highly specific goals. When they wanted programs that promoted innovations or protected their members' income and status, they did not really care which party gave them what they needed. They tried as best they could to work with both the Democrats and Republicans. Nor were the interest groups particularly worried about whether their programs were labeled liberal or conservative—just as long as they were passed. As a result, some of their most aggressive campaigns— the drive to establish a Federal Reserve System, for example— came to fruition as a liberal reform measure passed under Democratic leadership. It was President Woodrow Wilson who asked for and then signed the Federal Reserve Act of 1913. Other, similar laws—such as the Capper-Volstead Act, which encouraged American farmers to fix prices for their commodities—were introduced when conservative Republicans were in power. Little wonder then that the members of the new interest groups began to look to their lobbying organizations and not to a political party for what they wanted from the government. As this shift in allegiance took place, slowly and unevenly, the nature of politics in the United States was transformed.

This is not to say that reform along liberal or progressive lines was an insignificant development. During the years 1890–

1920, there were two important pulses of reform. The agrarian phase of this movement peaked in 1896, when William Jennings Bryan led the fused Democratic-Populist parties to a traumatic defeat. The second pulse, which was largely an urban and middle-class phenomenon, overlapped with populism. The progressive reformers began to seek changes in city and state governments in the 1890s; after the turn of the century, progressivism became a national movement under the leadership of presidents Theodore Roosevelt and Woodrow Wilson. In the realm of domestic politics, progressivism probably reached its peak in the years 1910–1914, when the federal government adopted a number of new measures drafted along liberal lines.

Reform had the important effect of encouraging the further development of interest groups. Many were organized to promote specific liberal innovations. Typical of these were the so-called Good Government organizations (nicknamed "Goo-Goos") that sought to wrest control of municipal politics from the hands of urban machines. In the states new groups such as the Milwaukee Municipal League in Wisconsin and the Ladies Health Protection Association in New York worked to achieve progressive ends in their respective states. On the national level there was a new National Municipal League, a National Child Labor Association, and a National Conference of Social Work, all dedicated to progressive ideals in government.

Where the more active government called for by the reformers seemed to threaten some faction's interests—as it usually did—the result was a counterreformation. Many businessmen formed or revitalized their associations. They revamped the National Association of Manufacturers and created a new United States Chamber of Commerce. Every industry now had to have its trade association and many supported several such organizations. A great wave of organizational activity swept through the United States in these years, bringing with it a political system that was markedly different from America's nineteenth-century form of democracy.

It was at this time that the democratic politics of parties began to give way to the broker-state politics of interest groups. Americans began to vote less often. No longer did it seem so absolutely vital to cast a ballot for your candidate or party. When your material interests and status were being protected by your pressure group, your firm, or your union, the trek to the voting booth began to seem superfluous—especially when the weather was bad. After particular governmental functions were insulated from partisan politics, as were the so-called independent regulatory commissions and some municipal governments, there was even less reason to support a political party. The ensuing decline in voter turnout and in party allegiance, which began at the turn of the century, continued for several decades. In 1896, three out of every four eligible voters had actually cast their ballots in the contest for the presidency. By 1920, less than half bothered to choose between Warren Gamaliel Harding and his Democratic opponent, James M. Cox.

As this was happening, the third and final partner in triocratic politics, the administrative state, was beginning to acquire a strong foothold in the United States. In local government, in state government, and at the federal level, Americans created a great variety of new bureaucratic agencies in the years 1890–1920 to perform tasks that had previously been left to the private sector or to chance. Some of these agencies grew up hand in hand with the new economic institutions. In these cases the government organizations from their origins sought the same goals of economic security and technical innovation that characterized the modern firm, profession, or farm group. In the U.S. Department of Agriculture during these years, just this sort of bureaucracy was evolving—side by side with the farm interest groups. By the end of World War I, the foundations of the farm triocracy were solidly laid, and this new system of government was producing results that pleased those agriculturists who were organized and politically effective. By that time, too, many other Americans could look to the same sorts of public-private triumvirates to protect their interests.

A number of the new government agencies were products of liberal reform, and that political ideology often shaped their performance, especially during their initial years. In the cities, reformers created new commissions to regulate transportation companies and protect the public's interests. State governments acquired similar controls over their electrical power and communications systems. In Washington, D.C., the Interstate Commerce Commission was revived from near death, given new powers, and sent forth to harness on behalf of the public the nation's most vital mode of transportation, the railroads.

Whatever their origins, however, these governmental bodies soon became closely affiliated with those new economic institutions that had the greatest direct interest in their operations. Some of these organizations were the very ones they were supposed to be regulating—the railroads or the power companies, for example; when this happened, the government agency was said to be "captured." But often the most influential organizations were those of the regulated firm's customers or suppliers. It was the shippers and farmers who exerted the most influence on the ICC around the time of the First World War. To win a struggle such as this, they had above all to be represented by effective interest groups. The full-time representatives of the groups were always there, doing the only job they had. They were often well financed, usually skillful, and always single-minded. The reformers who had originally sought the agency would usually lose interest in it as the years passed. But not the spokesmen for the pressure groups or corporations or unions. They were alert to the opportunities provided, for instance, when new administrations came into office and appointments to the departments and agencies had to be made. Gradually, they transformed many of these public bodies, giving them goals similar to those of the government institutions that had been created at their behest: the public interest, redefined, became the quest for security or the drive for technical innovation, the twin goals of the new economic institutions.

Regardless of which party was in power, regardless of whether liberals or conservatives were in the driver's seat, American government continued to grow and to evolve along these lines in the years that followed. In the 1920s, when presidents like Harding, Coolidge, and Hoover were in office and the nation was devoted to "normalcy," you might have expected this trend to be reversed, at least temporarily. It wasn't. The focal point merely shifted from the federal to the state and local levels. The total number of federal employees went down in the twenties, but state and local governments more than made up for that. If states like Maryland were going to control everything from chiropractors to plumbing, they needed more hands to do the job. By 1930 the United States had about three-quarters of a million more government employees than it had needed at the beginning of the decade. The development of our modern public bureaucracies was thus a much broader and more deeply rooted process than liberal reform or the maneuvers of party politics.

To many Americans, however, reform has seemed to be the prime mover of our political system. When I was growing up, my father frequently explained to me in blunt terms that our modern public bureaucracies all dated from the New Deal and the machinations of FDR. This idea is still popular in some circles in southern Indiana today. But obviously the statistics do not support that conclusion. When Herbert Hoover was still president, about seven percent of all the employed workers in the U.S. drew their paychecks from a government of some sort. Ten years later, on the eve of America's entry into World War II, a little more than eight percent of our employed workers were in the public sector.

By that time, the total figure for government employment was certainly impressive: it was 3,762,000 persons. Most of these employees worked in large public organizations—federal, local, or state—that were closely linked to various interest groups and to a legislative body of some sort. Fifty years of political change had given Americans a series of public bureaucracies strong enough to provide the third element in the new triocratic mode of politics.

During the Great Depression, most of the growth in government had taken place at the federal level and this helps explain my father's strong condemnation of the New Deal (and the equally one-sided evaluations of most liberal historians). Some of the reform measures of that era were driven home over fierce conservative opposition. The National Labor Relations Act, for example, aroused bitter antagonism among those business interests that were opposed to unionism in almost any form. They fought the unions and the NLRB through the courts and in the marketplace until the early forties. Then, at last, wartime prosperity and continued judicial support for this innovation finally undercut the opposition. Business interests adapted to the new situation, just as they had to other, similar liberal reforms.

A number of the other New Deal measures were of course easy for business leaders to accept because the laws had been introduced at their request. Businessmen and their representatives were the strongest advocates of the National Industrial Recovery Act (1933). The leading role in banking reform was played by the bankers themselves, and the Merchant Marine Act of 1936 merely upgraded the system of subsidies and price controls that the U.S. government had long been providing to its shipowners. Some of the country's largest corporations sought and supported government programs such as these and so did many of the nation's other new economic institutions. The agricultural interests, as we have seen, got what they wanted in Washington during the thirties, and so did the coal industry, the spokesmen for those druggists who were fighting chain stores, the truckers and bus companies, the dealers in securities, etc. Far from being anomalies in an era of reform, these arrangements were the typical product of the effort in twentieth-century America to adapt our system of government to the needs of a middle-aged society. By the end of the decade, that adaptation was far enough along that many Americans (including my father) properly sensed that politics in this country had been transformed in some irrevocable way. They were right. By 1940 the old system of democratic government had given way to triocracy. They were wrong, however, insofar as they (again, including my father) saw the new system as merely a liberal or progressive innovation, a child of the New Deal. Had it been that alone, the new form of government would not have represented such a decisive break with the past nor would it have been as durable as it subsequently proved to be.

IV

Triocracy lent to the American government a type of stability that it never before had possessed. The new institutional alliances were firmly planted in many cases. Good leadership, abundant funding, and mutuality of interests made these triumvirates difficult to uproot. Their stoutest defense was the fact that they were providing large groups of Americans with exactly what they wanted—and more and more of the country's citizenry were involved in some such political arrangement through their local, state, or federal government. Triocracies were as prevalent in our state governments as they were in Washington, D.C. Wherever bureaucracies, legislatures, and strong interest groups joined together, democratic government gave way to the new style of politics and our system of government became more stable.

People who regularly worked through their pressure groups rather than the political parties were not likely to provide support for a broad-gauged campaign aimed at undermining these alliances. An attack on other triocracies might endanger their own. Moreover, these were the persons who were by 1940 least attached to any party. Their party ties had been weakened by their dedication to the new system of politics. Protected by their pressure group, served by their governmental agency, assuaged by their friendly congressmen, they were satisfied with triocracy. They were not going to be foot soldiers in a battle to eliminate privilege for others—and certainly not for themselves. Their support, sometimes tacit and sometimes direct, contributed to the inertia that was to characterize American politics for many years to come. It was fitting that the middle-aged society thus became less flexible, politically less supple.

Partial compensation for this new degree of rigidity was provided by the emphasis in politics (as in the economy) on one particular form of change, that is, technical innovation. The country's political organizations were strongly influenced by this second major goal of America's intensive economy. In agriculture this meant promoting research and development at all levels of government. In the professions, state supported institutions financed research and promulgated the findings of those who were on the cutting edge of the discipline. Business looked to the political system for trained professional managers, for help in standardizing products and processes, for the scientific and technological personnel and knowledge essential to progress in this new setting. Labor sought government programs that would train or retrain workers displaced by technological innovations. Our political system was responsive to all of these demands.

In the late 1930s, however, all of these groups were also

looking to the government for something it could not yet provide. While the new structure of political economy could ensure that oil prices would remain relatively stable, that farmers would have parity in commodity prices, and that doctors would not face what they felt was unreasonable competition, the United States had, as yet, no means of ensuring that the aggregate level of economic activity would be high enough to protect the jobs of most workers or the incomes of most investors. The whole was still less than the parts. During the 1920s and 1930s, government leaders had experimented with a number of programs aimed at solving this problem. As late as 1940, however, there were still over eight million persons unemployed and the gross national product of the United States was only slightly above the level it had reached in 1929. Between 1929 and 1940, the economy had grown more slowly than the population, despite all that the Hoover administration and the New Deal had done. It remained for the Second World War to show Americans how they could use their new system of government to solve this particular problem.

5

HOT WAR, COLD WAR, AND THE NEW AMERICAN SYSTEM, 1941–1950

The first battleship to sink was the *Oklahoma*. Moored in Pearl Harbor on battleship row, the *Oklahoma* was hit by Japanese torpedoes in the first minutes of the surprise attack. The ship rolled over in the shallow water of the harbor, its superstructure rammed into the mud. Over four hundred men died on the *Oklahoma* and more than 1,000 on its sister ship *Arizona*, which exploded when a bomb struck its powder magazines. By the end of the attack on the morning of December 7, 1941, the battle line of the U.S. Pacific Fleet had been destroyed. It had taken about four years to build the *Oklahoma* and only a few minutes to destroy the ship. The entire attack lasted two hours, but in that time the navy and army lost 2,334 men and millions of dollars worth of equipment.

For America the war was tragic and costly from its first moments. By the time the nation had fully mobilized its forces and geared the economy to military production, the United States was spending $1.2 billion a week to defend itself. As late as 1937, America's total annual tab for national defense had been less than a billion dollars. To win this war, however, the country poured its human and material resources into the greatest military effort of its history.

In terms of their direct contribution to the domestic economy, these resources might just as well have been dumped into Lake Erie. The expensive planes and tanks and ships that America used to win the war were not useful or productive in any other sense. They drained the nation's economy, heavily taxing its ability to produce enough to meet the normal needs of its civilian population. Many of these needs were not met. They were deferred until the war was over.

But ironically, amidst the great destruction of the war, America prospered. By the end of 1942, with mobilization well under way, the country's gross national product had jumped from $124 to $158 billion, and unemployment had dropped from 9.9 to 4.7 percent of the work force. Deficit financing at levels the New Dealers had found unimaginable— let alone attainable—was spurring the national economy to a higher level of output and employment. The GNP increased by about thirteen percent during the first full year of the war. The American economy had soon surpassed the best level of output per capita achieved before the Great Depression, and in 1943 and 1944 the expansion was equally impressive. By the time Germany surrendered in 1945, the United States was producing more than it ever had before and those who had remained at home were cashing the best paychecks of their lives. The Second World War had accomplished what the New Deal had failed to achieve.

The prosperity of the 1940s trickled all the way down to Princeton, Indiana, where my father was able to move our family from a small house near the railroad shops to a much larger home on the north side of town. Having established a bridgehead on this, the Main Street frontier of Princeton's middle class, he was determined not to retreat to South Seminary Street again. During the day he ran a small machine shop that serviced Princeton's coal mine. In addition to his full-time job, he ran a cottage industry (welding parts for tanks) in the garage at night. The times were so good that he stopped complaining for a few years about the way the New Deal had ruined the United States. Even the wartime shortages of consumer goods could not tarnish the sense of prosperity and of righteous accomplishment that he and many other Americans had as a result of the war.

II

The World War II experiment with large-scale deficit financing also convinced many Americans that the federal government could now iron out those major fluctuations in the economy that had caused so much distress in the past. Many of the converts to this new outlook were in strategic positions in government or in the new economic institutions. Even before the war ended, they were preparing for a political campaign aimed at making stabilization of the economy an explicit goal of the federal government.

At the heart of this new approach to political economy were the ideas of the English economist John Maynard Keynes. During the depression of the thirties, Keynes had contended that economic recovery could be achieved in the United States by a stiff dose of deficit financing. The government spending, he said, would take the place of the private sector investment lost when the economy turned downward after 1929. Later, when the capitalist engine began to hum along at a faster clip, private investment would pick up and the government's role could be reduced.

Appropriate as these ideas might have been for a nation ground down by the Depression, the Keynesian dogma spread very slowly in the thirties. In 1935 Keynes published a book that set forth the economic theory on which his policy prescriptions were based. But *The General Theory of Employment, Interest and Money* did not immediately multiply the faithful. It was the kind of book that delights those mathematically gifted persons who join organizations that only admit mathematically gifted persons. Among economists—a profession that abounds with these gifted folks—the Keynesian concepts made faster inroads. By the late thirties, the ideas of the English economist were beginning to push aside the traditional theories of economics. Still, the Keynesians were only one faction in a profession that in the thirties had exerted very little influence on public policy.

The Second World War changed this situation drastically. When the country was forced to engage in heavy deficit financing and when the results were those that Keynes had predicted, this new outlook on the national economy quickly became the accepted theory of the economics profession. Moreover, professional economists found new allies among those who had substantial amounts of power in America. Keynesian ideas now won a broad following among the nation's organizational and governmental elites. Out in southern Indiana most of the people were oblivious to what was happening. But in the offices of the powerful and the boardrooms of the wealthy, new ideas were taking hold. Many of the most important leaders in our society were determined to see to it that ways were found to translate the new ideology into specific public policies that would stabilize the national economy— and, incidentally, protect their interests. Once again, private profit and the public welfare were happily meshed.

The Keynesian outlook had a great deal going for it. This new body of theory showed how, in specific terms, Americans could solve the problem of controlling and thus stabilizing the aggregate level of economic activity in the United States. Then, while the country's new economic institutions each sheltered the income of their respective members, the federal government could ensure that the total national income was large enough to go around. These new federal policies promised to keep the economy from sagging back into a depression at the end of the war. Little wonder, then, that

so many leaders of America's most powerful economic organizations and so many government officials were by the
war's end converts to this new creed.

The Keynesian approach had broad appeal in part because
it was an inherently conservative ideology and in part because
it was so well suited to triocratic government. It was conservative
because it provided a way to make modern capitalism—the
economy of great corporate entities—viable. Without some
sort of federal program that would prevent major depressions
like that of the thirties, the future of American capitalism
would have been dim. Keynesian fiscal policies, successfully
implemented, could turn aside the critiques of those who
sought more radical changes in the American economy. A
capitalist system with aggregate demand and employment
safely under control could have a secure future in the postwar
world.

The call for an active fiscal policy appealed to all three
of the partners in triocracy. The legislators would be favored
with larger budgets. Most of the new economic institutions
could support the general goal of economic stability and could
find means of achieving this objective consistent with their
own interests. Keynesianism was, after all, neutral about means
and about intermediate goals. The new policies could be used
to achieve full employment. Or to control inflation. Or to
promote a faster rate of growth. Or some combination of
these and other goals. A wide range of interests could thus
find something appealing in this sort of federal program.

By the end of the Second World War, considerations
such as these had generated substantial elite support for a
Keynesian policy. The leaders of many of the country's economic institutions were very nervous about the conversion
to a peacetime economy. Even the officers of some of the
nation's largest corporations—those that had fared rather
well in the thirties—wanted the national government to assume

this new responsibility. They joined the coalition supporting the Employment Act of 1946, the measure that institutionalized America's new national system of fiscal controls.

For a statute of such awesome proportions, the Employment Act introduced few structural innovations in American government. The president was provided with a new Council of Economic Advisers—to ignore or to listen to as he saw fit. The council provided a well-placed roost for some of the country's leading academic economists, but all they could do was suggest policies and analyze the economic implications of particular decisions. The president (who was now required to give the legislature a regular economic report) still decided what to propose and Congress (which was given a joint committee on the economic report) could still deal with the chief executive's budget and tax measures as it saw fit. The act did not even specify what the specific goal of the new federal policy would be. Instead, the law listed several possible objectives (including the promotion of "maximum employment, production, and purchasing power"), leaving the legislature to decide as it always had what brand of political economy the United States would actually have.

Still, the Employment Act of 1946 was far more significant than any of the reform or relief measures of the 1930s. For the first time in our history, the federal government's responsibility for the level of economic activity in this country was written into law. The president and Congress were mandated to exercise control over the largest and wealthiest economic system in the world. When Congress approved this bill on February 20, 1946, the command post of capitalism moved from Wall Street to Washington, D.C.

In the next few years, though, it began to look as if the economy might make it without any directives or fiscal stimulus from the nation's capital. The pent-up demand and the large accumulation of savings from the war years kept output and employment at high levels. The fears about reconversion soon wilted away. Millions of ex-servicemen were reabsorbed into the work force. Rosie the Riveter was eased back into her prewar line of work (sewing cotton blouses at the local clothing plant), and many of her coworkers were sent home to do those household chores that have traditionally earned them praise instead of income. These wholesale readjustments were not achieved without conflict, and during the early postwar years my father began to complain again about the New Deal, about the way Roosevelt and now Harry S Truman had ruined America, about the labor unions sent (I gathered) just to blight his life. From our present perspective, however, the reconversion seems to have been relatively smooth. Above all, it was managed without throwing the economy back into the deep depression so many had begun to worry about in 1944 and 1945.

As a result, the government could afford to abandon price controls and slash federal spending. Expenditures for national security dropped from over $81 billion in 1945 to $13 billion in 1948, but the private sector took up the slack. It was 1949 before the test came. Then, just as the country slid into its first major postwar recession, events overseas intruded again, decisively changing America's political economy.

Cold War tensions had started to breed higher military expenditures in 1949, and the following year the Korean War jolted spending for national security up to a new and significant level. From that point on, the government had a powerful fiscal lever that could be used to manipulate the economy. While the Employment Act of 1946 had given the federal government responsibility for the economy, it was Cold War spending for national defense from the late forties on that gave Washington the means of exercising that control. By 1950 the new system was firmly in place, sustained by a consensus among the American people and their leaders that the United States had to use its wealth and power to resist communist aggression around the world. This task was expensive. Eventually even America's great resources would be taxed too heavily. But in 1950, the U.S. economy was humming along, able to provide all of the guns that were needed abroad and the butter that was needed at home.

III

As this new national system of political economy was evolving, some very important changes were also taking place in the country's new economic institutions. In agriculture, for instance, the great public-private system for encouraging more efficient production began at last to pay off. All of the money spent on research, on experimental stations, on agricultural schools and scholars—all of those expenditures would not have survived an honest cost-benefit analysis as late as 1940. But then, suddenly, the entire agricultural sector began to change. County agents had been trying for years to persuade farmers to mend their ways, but with little success. Wartime demand, wartime prices, and a wartime shortage of labor did the trick. A great rush of innovations in the forties made American farming the wonder of the world. New fertilizers, seeds, breeding techniques, machinery, and farm organizations were at the heart of this transformation. Between 1940 and 1950, they enabled U.S. farmers to raise their productivity by sixty percent.

The scientific and technical knowledge that played a crucial role in this second agricultural revolution* came largely from the public, not the private, sector. Even the largest farms did not have their own research stations or labs. City dwellers paid for much of that research through their taxes. They

* Please don't fret if it slipped your mind that the first such revolution in productivity took place in the middle of the nineteenth century. Your high school history teacher probably forgot it too.

had for years supported the state and federal institutions that sponsored agricultural research, just as they paid for the system of price and production controls that had emerged in the 1930s. Now, in the forties the fruits of those investments were harvested when this complex public-private partnership began to yield astonishing results. By 1950 only twelve percent of the nation's work force was on the farm. But they were able to feed and (in part) clothe the rest of the population more efficiently than had ever been the case before, while producing a substantial surplus for export. Agriculture in this decade recorded just the sort of technical progress that was essential to a middle-aged economy that could no longer depend upon extensive growth.

The great corporations that dominated America's industrial economy also experienced a remarkable series of changes in the 1940s. At the beginning of the decade, most of these companies were highly centralized bureaucracies which concentrated on producing a relatively small line of closely related products or services. Usually the products were those made in similar ways from similar materials. The U.S. Steel Corporation was typical of this type of company. While U.S. Steel was a very large firm, with assets of about $2 billion, and while it made and marketed products ranging from very fine wire to the largest steel girders, most of its activities took place within the iron and steel industry. It would no more have ventured into aluminum production than a normal college professor would have doubled as a race car driver.

Some few companies had broken out of this mold before the Second World War. Firms like DuPont and General Electric had ventured beyond the confines of a single industry, making good use of their great technological capabilities to diversify their products. To corporations such as these the traditional boundaries of an industry began to have very little significance. By the end of the thirties, DuPont was manufacturing products as varied as heavy industrial chemicals and photographic film and firearms, as well as the explosives that had originally been its sole product.

In the 1940s diversification along these lines became the norm among the largest U.S. companies. Wartime profits provided the capital for expansion. Investments in R & D began to yield the charts that management could follow as they steered their firms toward a more secure future. By diversifying, these giant firms freed themselves from the growth path of a single industry. As demand for one of their products leveled off, they could shift their resources to a faster-growing sector of the economy. Diversification expanded the firm's horizons, placing a premium on flexible, innovative leadership.

The old style of highly centralized business bureaucracy was too rigid to cope with the complex situations created by diversification. In the early years of big business in this country, men like Andrew Carnegie, John D. Rockefeller, and Henry Ford had been able to dominate their business empires, tightly grasping the lines of authority that reached from the board room to the factory floor. As the moguls passed away, their places had been taken by committees of committeemen, less interesting fellows than the tycoons but men who continued to tug at those long lines of power and communications reaching from the top to the bottom of the firm. When a business diversified, however, the managers could no longer exercise that kind of direct control. The business, or better, the several businesses of the large firm were just too complex to be administered efficiently by a centralized organization. Those managers who tried soon found red ink on their balance sheets.

The managers of these firms adopted a more efficient, decentralized style of organization. The decentralized firm resembled a series of separate businesses, joined at the top by a central office which commanded the flow of capital and evaluated the performances of its highly varied constituent divisions. Each of these divisions enjoyed a relatively high degree of autonomy, which enabled them to respond to the particular demands created by their product lines, services, or the territory they commanded.

The decentralized corporation proved to be efficient in running a diversified enterprise spread over a very broad geographical area. In the postwar years companies of this sort were the ones that most often ventured overseas to do business. Some U.S. businesses had been operating in other countries long before the Second World War. But after 1945, many more looked overseas for markets, for raw materials, and for inexpensive labor. When U.S. capital went abroad in this form, it was accompanied by U.S. managers and U.S. technology—both of which were needed in the aftermath of the most destructive war in history. In this way, the decentralized, multinational firm promoted postwar reconstruction while it protected itself from fluctuations in the American economy. If demand leveled off at home, the U.S.–centered multinational could merely shift its interest and investments to one of several countries overseas.

By 1950 the American business corporation had been transformed. The model firm was diversified across several industries, decentralized in structure, and either heavily committed overseas or seriously considering such a move. In the short space of ten years, the mood of our corporate leaders had been completely reversed. The caution and conservatism of the depression years had given way to a widespread optimism about the country's economic prospects. The flexible, high-technology firms seemed from that perspective to have made a remarkably successful accommodation to the basic needs of America's mature, intensive economy.

Labor leaders could also chortle a bit about their accomplishments in the 1940s. As the wheels of the war economy began to spin at a faster pace, employers stopped worrying about fighting the unions and became concerned above all with keeping up production. Cost-plus government contracts took the pressure off wages. The labor unions worked hand in hand with their favorite congressmen to keep wage controls in friendly hands. In this favorable setting the nation's unions were able to recruit many new members and to consolidate their power in the labor market. Between 1940 and 1945 the unions added about 5,800,000 new members to their rolls.

After the Japanese surrendered and the pace of demobilization quickened, the unions had to struggle hard to hold onto these gains. In the 1920s they had failed to do this, and the labor movement had suffered a severe setback. Not so in the late forties.* In spite of the passage of the Taft-Hartley Act in 1947—a measure the unions fiercely condemned—and in spite of public concern about communist infiltration of the unions, and in spite of embarrassing investigations of union corruption, the labor movement held its own in the postwar years. In 1950 almost one-third of the nonagricultural work force was organized, and the unions had a tight grip on the labor markets in such strategic industries as transportation and communications.

By that time, too, it was clear that laborers—organized or not—had been able to preserve many of the economic gains they had made during the Second World War. A significant redistribution of income in favor of the laboring classes had taken place while America was struggling against

* My father gave the family frequent lectures on this subject. Our evening meals were the occasion for these fierce attacks on the union with which he had to deal, on the shop steward who headed that organization, and on the late Franklin D. Roosevelt, who was held personally responsible for most of the problems that arose at my father's small machine shop. Even though I was dumb as a gourd and was preoccupied with the fortunes of our local football team (and one of its cheerleaders), I sometimes wondered how one man could have done that much to change such a large nation as ours. But alas, my father did not have a question and answer session after his lectures, and I had to wait some years before I found the right answer to this question.

the Axis powers. This was the first such redistribution in the twentieth century. It was a direct result of the shortage of labor that developed during the war. The war economy did what the New Deal had not been able to accomplish, shifting some of the nation's income away from those who owned our factories and toward those who worked in them. Economic conditions after the war were good enough to enable labor to maintain this new and more favorable position.

The war had also quickly improved conditions for those middle-class professionals who had been so concerned about choking off entry to their trades during the depression. As the economy surged ahead, the demand for professional expertise of all kinds greatly exceeded the supply. Engineers were needed in the armed services and defense industries. Doctors were scarce. Many professional schools were hard pressed to keep going as young men and women were drawn off to military service, and for a time this sharply reduced the number of young persons embarking on professional careers.

The surprising growth of the economy in the late forties did the same thing for professionals that it did for factory workers. Indeed, some professions in great demand were now actually better off than they had been during the war. This was true for engineers in many industries and for scientists. The pressures of a growing, technologically advanced economy encouraged many of the professional schools to expand and upgrade their programs. Returning servicemen had to be trained. State and local governments pumped more and more tax dollars into these programs, invigorating research as well as education in many of the professions.

The most dramatic change in this decade involved the federal government's new role in the development of scientific and technical knowledge. During the early forties, the United States harnessed its research personnel and resources to the war effort. Federal dollars poured into basic and applied research, energizing the scientific and engineering professions that serviced these projects. The most awesome breakthrough came in atomic energy. The bomb symbolized for most Americans the advent of a new era, one in which scientific innovations might well become the primary force reshaping society. If so, it seemed prudent to ensure that the United States would be the leader in generating those ideas and their practical applications.

In the years 1945–1950 the country did exactly that. By 1947, the federal government was already spending $625 million a year to promote research and development in this country. At first much of this work was directed by the newly founded Atomic Energy Commission, by the Office of Naval Research, by the National Institutes of Health, and other agencies. In 1950, Congress capped this diverse structure with a National Science Foundation "to develop and encourage the pursuit of a national policy for the promotion of basic research and education in the sciences." The United States was by that time as heavily committed to the development of new ideas in the scientific, medical, and engineering professions as it had been in 1940 to the promotion of agricultural innovations. With some luck, the NSF and its sister agencies might see their efforts through to the sort of dramatic conclusion that the Department of Agriculture could point to in 1950.

Changes such as those taking place in these modern professions were occurring throughout American society in the forties. Wartime growth and postwar expansion helped the new economic institutions put down deep roots. Where it seemed necessary (and it usually did), they kept the protective arrangements they had carefully put together in the public and private sectors before 1940. In farming, for example, the second agricultural revolution did not convince cotton growers that they should abandon price and production controls. Nor did the most technologically advanced and diversified corporations go out of their way to stir up price competition with other giant firms. Where triocracies were protecting the income and status of particular groups, they emerged intact from this decade of astonishing changes.

In the postwar years, in fact, some of our public bureaucracies began to show signs that they were maturing into very formidable institutions in their own right. They began to conduct a form of diplomatic relations with one another, like nation-states. They established alliances and concluded formal pacts and understandings. The Joint Chiefs of Staff, acting on behalf of their respective services, held the domestic counterpart of a series of international conferences when they met first at Key West, Florida, and later at Newport, Rhode Island, in 1948. The agreement (that is, the peace treaty) that they signed enabled the country to get on with the task of rearming for the Cold War—a process that had been stymied by fundamental disagreements between the navy, the army, and the air force. Similarly, the Treasury Department and the Federal Reserve System were able in 1950 to sign a treaty, called the Accord, which specified their respective roles in handling the nation's fiscal and monetary policies. Interbureaucratic diplomacy of this sort had taken place before World War II, but in the forties it became a more common practice and the resulting agreements assumed a more important role in shaping America's public policies.

So formidable were the powers of our public and private institutions that our middle-aged society now needed effective leadership more than it had ever before in its history. The officers of our modern organizations had substantial discretionary authority. They could, when all else failed, dig in their heels and resist change, exercising a kind of veto on innovations that seemed to threaten the interests of their particular organization. But the country often could not afford stalemates of this sort. The American people had brought significant parts of their society—including now the national economy—under control. They badly needed farsighted and effective leaders at the helm. They needed men and women who could make the new American system run if the United States was going to continue to prosper in the years ahead.

<h1 style="text-align:center">IV</h1>

So my father was both right and wrong about what had happened to America. He was wrong to look to FDR as the major agent of change and the New Deal as the most decisive watershed in our history. The New Deal did more to round out an already existing structure of new political and economic organizations than it did to redirect our government or revamp our fundamental institutions. Developments of those proportions took place, as we have seen, in the 1940s, not during the Great Depression. They were eased into place by the shoehorn of prosperity, which probably explains why my father and other Americans didn't sense exactly how much their lives were being changed until near the end of that decade.

The transformation did take place, however, and about that my father was right. He saw how radically different our society was in the late 1940s. The creation of a new national system to control the level of economic activity was awesome in itself. Couple that with the important developments that had occurred in the country's most basic economic institutions, and you have a decade of startling and unsettling innovations. These transitions disturbed my father, but he should have been happier than he was about the way America was entering middle age. After all, he and his family had been able to hang on to their perch in Princeton's middle class. Nor was he alone.

In southern Indiana and elsewhere in the country Americans were showing remarkable flexibility about the changes taking place. They complained a great deal, but they were doing a rather good job of balancing America's need for security against its need for continued innovation. Prosperous and strong in 1950, the nation could afford to celebrate the creation of its new American system of political and economic institutions.

6

MAKING THE SYSTEM WORK,
1950–1968

He comes to your cocktail party wearing his bermuda shorts and of course his running shoes. You're afraid of what will follow, but you ask, "How's the running going, Sam?" It's hard not to ask. The dirty, scuffed shoes stand out. They lure you into this conversation even though Sam's drive to conquer the marathon is the last thing you want to talk about this afternoon, or any afternoon. Sam is skinny and you are, well, heavy. Maybe a little fat. You and Sam are both forty-seven, but he runs six miles a day and you get out of breath if you hurry back to the grill to turn over the hamburgers. Sam exhausts you just talking about his plans. Running. A new job. A clever vacation. Whatever. Sam is always pushing against life while you sit in the middle of it and float.

But whether you are Sam or Fred the Floater, you have problems. The middle-aged jock, Sam, is always on the verge of overextending himself. He pushes that right calf muscle a bit further than it will go. He knocks a few more seconds off his best time, even though the temperature is in the high nineties. He tells you about the injuries (fairly often) and wears his knee brace like a medal of honor. But one of those hot summer days it may be something more vital than his right knee or his hamstring that gives out. Fred's problem is just the opposite. He wants to float in the same place every day. He would be happy bobbing up and down on a still lake, quietly building up fat in his cardiovascular system, without a worry. But life keeps churning up the waters and the winds keep shifting. He gets anxious—and with good cause. Even the flabbiest floater has to paddle now and then just to get the waves out of his face.

The challenge at middle-age is to find a way to steer between these two extremes. That, alas, is more difficult than it sounds for either the middle-aged person or the middle-aged society. Both would do well to avoid overextending themselves. The United States of the postwar era was, like Sam and his friend, no longer quite as flexible, as resilient as it once was. The powerful institutions of this century had put down deep roots that enabled them to resist change. The young society had been able to look past each fresh blunder to a new frontier. The margin for error had still been rather large. The middle-aged society could not escape in that way; it carried a heavier burden of obligations and had to live with its mistakes (often far longer than Americans like). But floating was dangerous too. As the national and international contexts changed, America and its new institutions had to keep adjusting, fighting off the desire to stay in one place. Where these institutions were very large bureaucratic organizations, they had to struggle against the kind of built-in inertia that characterizes such systems whether they are in the private or the public sector. Neither stasis nor frantic activity was the right prescription for a middle-aged nation that needed prudent leadership if it was to remain successful in a rapidly changing postwar world.

II

When leadership is mentioned, our minds usually leap to the presidency, but my concern here is with leadership at all levels of the postwar society. In the country's new economic institutions, good leadership was needed just as badly as it was in the White House or on Capitol Hill. Each of these institutions had to respond to changes in its immediate environment, developments that frequently threatened the private and public arrangements that protected the income and status of the institution and its members. The means of generating innovation had to be kept running smoothly. These leaders had to do more than merely react to obvious pressures. They had to anticipate future developments that would impinge on their organizations. It was dangerous to float for very long. While the tempo of change had slowed in middle-aged America, our society was far from static. Moreover, the international context, which was now far more important to the United States than it had ever been before, was changing in dramatic ways in the years following World War II. The leaders of the new economic institutions frequently found themselves forced to take positions on revolutionary developments far from their customary locus of operations at home. It was a demanding environment, one that thoroughly tested the leadership of the country's most powerful organizations.

Least successful of all the elites in meeting these challenges were the country's labor leaders. Their organizations had experienced an astonishing increase in power and wealth during the previous decade. All too many of the country's labor officials responded to this bounty in the traditional American style—that is, by wallowing in corruption. A series of investigations uncovered a record of racketeering, bribery, and theft that would have done justice to Jay Gould, the nineteenth-century robber baron of the railroads, or to Boss

Tweed, who pilfered his money from the city of New York at about the same time. These comparisons are useful. They should remind us that with one significant exception,* every American institution that has experienced a phase of very rapid expansion in power and wealth has had to contend with widespread corruption among its leaders. But as time passed, most of the institutions managed to overcome these initial problems. While they never eliminated corrupt practices entirely, they at least made them the exception, not the rule. The swashbuckling phase of dishonesty normally lasted for less than a generation. It was organized labor's particular disadvantage that this initial wave of corruption crested just as the labor movement was facing other serious problems.

The greatest challenge came from the industrial economy, where employment was beginning to level off. These were the kinds of workers who were the mainstay of America's labor unions. For most of the twentieth century, factory work had been growing rapidly. But now the growth rate in that part of the economy was slowing down. Technological advances were reducing the demand for the old style of factory worker. The new jobs in the United States were increasingly in the services sector. White-collar employment was growing fast. But the unions found it difficult to organize these workers, especially those in clerical jobs. As a result, the growth in total union membership slowed to a snail's pace, and the percentage of the work force that was unionized actually began to decline. Labor's leadership, hounded about corrupt practices and struggling hard just to hold the gains achieved before 1946, was unable to cope successfully with the problems it was facing in the economy and in politics. The leaders of American labor tried to float. But the winds continued to blow against them and their organizations.

Although much concern was expressed in those years

---

*I will tell you which one it was later.

about labor's political clout, the unions in the fifties and sixties were hard pressed just to hang on to the political position they had in 1950. They were unable to better that position significantly, by repealing the Taft-Hartley Act for instance. Taft-Hartley had been designed to swing the balance of public power away from the unions and toward their employers. It was in that sense successful. But if you bother to read the act (1947) today, it seems far from harsh, certainly not vindictively antilabor. The provision for an eighty-day cooling off period when a strike threatens the public interest will probably not make you shed a tear for the downtrodden worker. Why get excited about cooling off? Why worry about a regulation prohibiting labor organizations from coercing employees, refusing to bargain collectively, or charging excessive membership fees? But to the labor leaders of the forties and fifties, provisions such as these seemed to substitute paternalistic statism for collective bargaining. The true motive behind the act, said George Meany of the AFL, was "to return to the medieval concept of master and servant, with the master arbitrarily commanding and the servant meekly submitting." Fired by this vision, organized labor campaigned hard against the new measure. But to no purpose. Labor could not muster a strong enough coalition to repeal Taft-Hartley. It failed to achieve its goal in the fifties when the Republican resurgence built new roadblocks in labor's path. It failed again in the sixties, when the Democratic recovery seemed to have cleared the way for organized labor.

As the union leaders recognized, labor's triocracy was changing in the postwar years as the National Labor Relations Board matured. Like other new government agencies, the NLRB had begun its career in a somewhat nebulous position. For years, in fact, there had been strong suspicions that the agency would be struck down by the Supreme Court. Even after those fears had been quashed, the board had moved slowly in developing, case by case, issue by issue, its own new role in the nation's industrial relations. In the postwar years the outlines of that role were clarified and the agency became a stronger advocate of its own special position vis-à-vis the labor movement. Frequently the NLRB, in its mature and more forceful state, alienated the unions. Labor leaders reacted by expressing the fear that they had lost some of the protection they thought their organizations had acquired with the passage of the Wagner Act in 1935. They were right.

Other federal bureaucracies were also coming of age in the fifties and sixties. They too were gradually becoming more independent, were exerting more of their own influence on government policies. Thus the Social Security Administration began to have a great deal to do with the manner in which Congress modified the welfare system. Some regulatory agencies began to loosen the ties that had held them captive to the industries they ostensibly regulated. Where this happened, the other two partners in the triocratic alliances had to do some political scurrying to protect their interests. The leaders of the labor movement tried to do this in the fifties and sixties, but failed.

Labor's men of power found plenty of waves splashing in their faces. Corporations were creating new systems of labor relations that in many cases diminished the appeal of the unions. In political campaigns, the unions could not deliver their members' votes. When the labor leaders looked to Washington, D.C., for help, they all too often saw hostile faces at the Justice Department and Labor Department, as well as the NLRB. In the sixties, the unions threw their support behind the civil rights movement. But even the liberal friends of organized labor began to abandon ship when the nation's unions dragged their heels about opening their own ranks to black workers. In general the labor movement took a very conservative stance toward the vigorous efforts of organized blacks, and later, women, to gain access to unionized jobs that had heretofore been denied to them. By the late sixties, the labor movement had suffered significant losses in public support, due in large measure to the unions' weak leadership. Membership was declining. Where the leadership was more aggressive, it was all too often corrupt, as was the case with the Teamsters, and in many unions a deep gulf began to develop between the union members and their officers. The complaints of the members struck a responsive chord among all those citizens who had looked to labor's leadership for help in making the new American system work.

III

The leaders of America's agricultural institutions compiled a better record of performance in the postwar years. Of course they had less to fear than labor from changes in the public sector, in part because the sort of technological and economic trends that were working to labor's disadvantage were in the fifties and sixties highly favorable to American agriculture. The revolution in production that had begun during the Second World War and had carried through the late forties continued at an accelerating pace through the 1950s and the 1960s. By the end of the latter decade, there were, in effect, two separate agricultural economies in the United States: one consisted of large farms using substantial amounts of capital and advanced production techniques; the other, which included the majority of the farms in the country, consisted of relatively small, undercapitalized units using outdated techniques. Most of the nation's agricultural output came from the small number of farms in the first category. They were the ones that made our agriculture the most productive in the world and that prompted Russian visitors to tramp around in midwestern corn fields looking for the secret of the U.S. farm.

All of this happened while the most efficient farms— some of them giant agribusinesses—were continuing to make good use of the public-private system for controlling prices and production. Reformers with an eye to equity and college freshmen taking an introductory course in government find this hard to accept. Shouldn't the public benefits, they ask, have gone to the small, marginal farmers who needed them the most? If the controls and subsidies were the country counterpart of unemployment benefits, why were they going to the large, profitable interests? At times, even wise and powerful men of a conservative bent have asked this same question, and then the leaders of our agricultural organizations have had to labor extra hours to defend their power and the public funds that are funneled into agriculture's triocracies. The money is not a negligible consideration. In the 1950s, for instance, the federal government pumped about $5 billion into agriculture.

This money attracted some attention, and after Dwight David Eisenhower became president in 1953, he tried to turn off the spigot. After all, the farm sector was prosperous. The nation's most efficient farmers were doing very well. A new farm policy seemed to be called for, and Secretary of Agriculture Ezra Taft Benson was determined to see to it that marketing and acreage controls no longer prevented America's farmers from competing freely.

The farmers had other ideas. Even without the support of the secretary of agriculture, the leaders of the farm organizations were able to beat back this well-intentioned effort to go back to the old style of competitive enterprise. Working closely with Congress, and at times with bureaucrats within Benson's own department, the farm organizations won their battle. Far from cutting the funds going into agriculture, Eisenhower and Benson found themselves presiding over an increase in federal spending for price supports and production controls.

Having successfully thwarted this challenge to triocracy, the farm combine was able in the sixties to restore order and stability to its triple alliance. The top and bottom of the Department of Agriculture (by this time certainly a very mature bureaucracy) were brought back into agreement. The department abandoned any effort to change the farmers' new economic institutions. In the sixties the emphasis in farm policy was placed on disposing of the surplus churned out by America's wonderfully productive agricultural sector, and the disposal was managed in ways that maintained prices and profits. While the number of farm voters in the nation had continued to dwindle, agriculture's leaders had more than held their own in the struggle over public policy. They had curbed and brought back under control the top echelons of a federal bureaucracy that had for a time sought to change the balance of power in agriculture. They had improved and strengthened their new system of controls while their farmer clients were introducing truly remarkable changes in technique and organization. The economic changes made agriculture more efficient and more productive. The political maneuvers ensured that nothing would keep the nation's most successful farmers from harvesting the profits of those innovations.

IV

Most of the professions also enjoyed favorable economic conditions in the fifties and sixties. The expansion of the economy increased the demand for professional services; in many cases, in fact, the demand for services grew much faster than the nation's aggregate growth rate because of the increasing sophistication of our highly organized, urban society. The institutions that trained professionals reacted very slowly to the market. They were nevertheless growing during these years, as federal and state governments targeted more and more tax dollars for higher education. Support for research increased rapidly. By the mid-sixties federal support alone was over $15 billion a year. In one field, biomedical research, the appropriations for the National Institutes of Health and the National Institute of Mental Health grew between the late 1950s and the end of the sixties at a compounded annual rate of twenty-four percent. This public support energized research in science, engineering, and a number of other professions.

The sixties in particular were flush times in the academic breeding grounds of the professions. Teachers colleges transformed themselves into universities. Universities became multiversities. Not many college presidents had the nerve (or foresight) to tell their trustees that they were not turning the old school into the Harvard of the West. The Southwest. The Midwest. The Northwest. Every school with aspirations had to have its own doctoral mill and every vigorous dean had to see to it that the mill ran full tilt. In some cases they overloaded the market. For a time the United States actually had too many engineers. After the federal grant money leveled off and then began to decline, there were too many scientists around for the academic system to absorb. Professional historians—to bring the matter close at hand—became a glut on the market.*

The norm, however, was closer to the medical than the academic professions. America's doctors, for example, were never plagued by the historians' lemminglike urge to commit economic suicide by stuffing the market with too many competitors. The country's M.D.s skillfully defended the high standards of their craft in a way that left them enjoying increases in income that far exceeded the rate of inflation.

The medical professions were almost too successful. The public demand for a more forceful role for government in the field of medicine grew stronger in these two decades. If the labor unions were floating like Fat Fred, then the medical

*Because of tenure regulations, this sort of overproduction created problems largely for young academics looking for jobs, not for the full professors responsible for the glut.

organizations were behaving like Sam the Marathon Man; they overtaxed the public's tolerance, endangering their very favorable long-run position for immediate gains. The managers of most giant corporations had long ago learned not to do this. But America's doctors (with the exception of course of my brother-in-law) appear to have been blinded by the profession's own emphasis on its unique ability to understand and set policy for medical care. Medicine, like every other established profession, has a "mystery," a body of knowledge that sets its members off from the rest of society. The profession's status, power, and wealth depend in part on the extent to which society accepts the fact that such a mystery exists. When the professionals themselves begin to believe in this too strongly, however, they can develop the sort of self-righteous attitudes that characterized the American Medical Association in these years.

The result, in the sixties, was a serious political threat to the profession's power to control its own affairs. As is customary in American politics, the assault was oblique, aimed in this case at the need to provide less expensive medical attention for the elderly and the needy. But the Medicaid and Medicare plans actually posed a very general threat to the profession's autonomy and to its highly successful system of controls. For one thing, these proposals would have shifted important decisions about medical policy from the state level, where the doctors generally had things under control, to the federal level, where the profession's power was less secure. Then too, the new policies might only be the entering wedge. In the AMA's vision of the future, any federal intervention today was inevitably the first step toward the worst outcome possible: SOCIALIZED MEDICINE.

Spurred by these fears, the profession fought back. Through well-financed and well-managed campaigns, it was able to shape the new programs to suit its needs, without, however, preventing any federal action whatsoever. In their final form the new laws (1965) left a significant amount of authority where it had been all along, in the hands of doctors and state officials. The results were a tribute to the profession's resilience, high income, and political skill, and the outcome in this instance did not really endanger the profession's public-private system of economic controls. But the moral of the story was that professionals could afford neither to float along nor to seek their self-interest with such zeal as to alienate the public.

Other professions in America had similar experiences during these two decades, although in general they were not challenged as severely as medicine was. For the most part, they were able to hold their own economically and politically, although their leaders did not display any particular knack for anticipating problems. They were less hostile than union leaders to the demands for entry from blacks and women, but not much. None of the major professions compiled a record that would have convinced an unbiased observer that political pressure to knock down the barriers to entry was entirely unwarranted. The professional schools dragged their feet on admissions; they were even slower to eradicate the subtler forms of prejudice that could so powerfully undercut the performance of aspiring young black and female practitioners. The professions were conservative. They gave ground slowly and grudgingly, long after women had taken for themselves a new and significant role in the American work force. They were even slower to open their doors to those black Americans who were mounting a forceful campaign during these years to achieve equality of opportunity.

V

Corporate enterprise was also sluggish during the fifties and sixties in responding to the major social changes taking place in this country. American businesses were no more prepared to anticipate the new demands of blacks than were the professions or labor unions. Our great corporate combines resisted change, dragging their feet while pressure mounted for a political program that would open the doors to management for qualified blacks. Many of these corporations had long been employing blacks, but only as laborers. Advancement within the firm had remained a tortuous process, if it was possible at all. The percentage of black managers in America's leading businesses had remained woefully low through most of this century.

The same type of barriers stood in the way of women who sought business careers, in spite of the fact that some very successful businesswomen had already been able to get to the top by way of ownership. A few others had made it without this advantage, but their numbers had remained very small. Corporate management in the 1950s was still as overwhelmingly white and male as the golf courses frequented by the moguls.

As the winds of change mounted, America's business leaders managed at least to keep their corporations from foundering. During the sixties, in particular, pressures from interest groups and the government brought down some of the barriers to minority advancement. Actually the largest corporations, with their heavy emphasis upon measurable performance, proved to be more responsive to these pressures than smaller businesses in which a family or a single owner held sway. Often the very largest firms were running ahead of the professional schools in this regard. Once blacks and women were able to fight their way into and through the professional schools, they found access to lower-level managerial positions coming open in the sixties. All the barriers were not toppled, by any means. Once inside the door, the minority executive still found the route to the top littered with prejudices that were as hard to detect from outside as they were to avoid once you were inside the firm. Progress was slow and frequently frustrating. These were difficult times both for the firms and for those blacks and women who no longer were satisfied with the bottom rung of the ladder.

During these two decades, the country's businesses were far more successful in accommodating changes in their economic than in their social environment. Venturing more often into international operations, the combines found raw materials not available in the United States and new markets to supply. Among the largest firms, multinational operations became the norm during the fifties and sixties. While the domestic market still accounted for the great majority of the nation's goods and services, America's corporations now established important beachheads throughout the world. By the end of the sixties, the Ford Motor Company had subsidiaries in thirty-four different countries, from South Africa to Malaysia, from Belgium to Brazil. There were about twice as many Ford employees overseas as there were in the United States. Many other firms had substantial percentages of their assets in other countries. Equipment manufacturers like Black & Decker, food producers like H. J. Heinz, and communications firms such as ITT were heavily involved in other national economies.

These multinational firms were less vulnerable to economic fluctuations and their long-term futures were more assured than the nationally oriented businesses of the previous century. For one thing, the multinationals were partially insulated from the effects of the business cycle in the United States. They could shift capital from one country to another, taking advantage of the best opportunities for profitable investments. While American workers had reason to complain, the international firm protected its capital over the long term by seeking faster growing or less competitive markets than it could find at home. When our government was able to negotiate reductions in trade barriers, U.S. companies moved quickly into the newly opened markets in Europe and elsewhere in the world.

These same types of corporations continued to diversify their operations abroad and at home. The conglomerates of these years brought together highly varied activities under one corporate roof. No longer did these operations necessarily share common technologies or marketing techniques. To the casual observer, the combinations seemed now to make little sense. How could a company manufacturing bowling balls use its expertise to produce and distribute processed foods? Could textiles and rental automobiles and insurance actually be meshed in a profitable way? The answer in both cases was "yes." What was common to all of these ventures was the need for effective top-level management. This the decentralized firm could provide, along with capital, some political clout, and technical expertise.

The technical knowledge came from three sources, one of which was normally the large firm's own research and development program. In these years R & D expenditures by American companies climbed steadily, and by 1965, there were 375,500 scientists and engineers working in U.S. industry. The total industry expenditures for R & D that year were over $14 billion. This research helped some companies protect their current market position by giving them patents on related products and methods of production. More important were the opportunities for growth generated by industrial laboratories. These giant corporations could afford to make very large investments in research and could, if necessary, work on a major innovation for many years. They also had two other major sources of technical knowledge: they had the funds to buy new ideas from individuals and smaller companies; and during these years they benefited from government-sponsored research. All three sources combined in the fifties and sixties to make U.S. firms extremely efficient and innovative. Heavy investments in research went hand in hand with increases in productivity. Between 1950 and 1968, U.S.

productivity increased at an annual rate of 2.2 percent. These increases were vital to the growth of America's intensive, modern economy.

VI

The federal government, as well as industry, could take some of the credit for this performance. On balance, our political leaders were able to achieve the major goal of America's new national system of political economy. That objective was to stabilize the economy, to prevent those major downturns that had characterized our brand of capitalism from the early nineteenth century through the 1930s. We achieved that end. Whether our leaders were Democrats or Republicans, whether our country was at peace or at war, we did not sag into another Great Depression. There were economic problems. But even these difficulties cannot obscure the fact that the new institutions of the postwar era were clearly preferable to the system they had replaced. That was why only antediluvian conservatives wanted to talk about returning to the status quo ante-bellum.

Compare for a moment the record of America's economic performance in the 1950s and 1960s with the twenties and thirties. Don't tell me this is unfair because there was a Great Depression after 1929! The 1930s should be included for exactly that reason. Similar depressions had taken place about every generation before World War II. We need to compare our performance with and without such severe downturns. When we do, the record of the postwar era looks rather good. In the two decades before World War II the nation's growth rate (in GNP) had averaged 2.5 percent a year; gross national product per capita went up from $1,315 to $1,720. In the postwar, stabilized economy the growth rate was 3.6 percent per year, and per capita GNP jumped from $2,342 in 1950 to $3,555 in 1970 (all in constant dollars). The productivity of the new system was increasing faster than it had before the war too. In these several regards, the new American system was working very well indeed.

But the postwar experiences can tell us more than that. They can also show us what two distinctive styles of political leadership could do for this new set of institutions. For the first and more moderate style we can look to the two administrations of President Dwight David Eisenhower. When Eisenhower took office in January 1953, the economy was overheated. The Korean War, which had begun in June 1950, had spurred heavy buying in the private sector, followed by a dramatic increase in government expenditures. The government's share of America's GNP had jumped from about seven percent to over fifteen percent in the early fifties. With the economy already operating at close to full employment before the heavy wartime expenditures started, prices shot upward once the war began.* The government responded with a price and wage freeze, but the damage had already been done.

Under Eisenhower's leadership, the rate of federal spending was cut sharply and the inflationary pressures reduced in the mid-fifties. Through the rest of the decade, his administrations struggled, sometimes successfully and sometimes not, to keep a balanced budget. In a triocracy, however, the most determined executive can exhaust himself beating against well-entrenched interests. The unsuccessful attempt to change farm policy in the fifties showed how durable the new economic institutions could be.

Eisenhower's efforts to restructure the military establishment provide an even more telling example. In this case the chief executive seemed to hold all the trump cards: his detailed knowledge of military affairs, his reputation as a successful military leader, and his popularity with the voters

*The price increases were in this case largely in anticipation of future shortages.

should, it seems, have given him the power to override any resistance to his plans to improve the efficiency of the American military. Not so. The services were able to resist the frontal attack of their own commander in chief. Eisenhower was forced at last to settle for a partial victory. He was able to strengthen the hand of the secretary of defense and to shift the emphasis of our strategic planning and defense spending from traditional weapons systems to modern nuclear arms. His new look trimmed down the U.S. Army and restrained the navy's most ambitious plans for expansion. But even Eisenhower could not achieve the degree of unification that he sought in the military. He tried to short-circuit the services by stressing the role of the joint commands. But while this new order reduced the authority of the services, the navy, air force, and army retained far more power than Eisenhower had wanted them to have. The compromise was a good measure of how difficult it is in a triocracy for the chief executive actually to rein back on the political institutions he ostensibly directs.

Eisenhower nevertheless ground away steadily at a number of the public-private combines. As he left office, he warned the American people about one such coalition, which he identified as the military-industrial complex. He might well have pointed to others, as subsequent presidents have. Together, these combines and their constituent institutions exerted a steady upward pressure on both federal expenditures and on prices and wages. By resisting their pressures relentlessly for eight years, Eisenhower was able to hold his own. Even then, near the end of his second term, inflationary pressures mounted.

America's modern system of political economy had a built-in propensity for inflation. Each group which had organized effectively and achieved a measure of control over its economic fate was prepared to resist any downturn in its own income. Each eagerly awaited the opportunity to improve its position. The great corporations that produced most of our goods, the unions that defended the interests of employees, the associations that served our professionals, the farm organizations and other trade groups—all pressed for increases in the prices of the goods and services essential to their income and status. Many of the same institutions were deeply embedded in America's triocratic government. Here too they relentlessly sought advantages which either increased expenditures or decreased revenues—or both.

The new institutional structure thus prevented the kind of severe deflation that had taken place in the Great Depression of the 1930s. But the price of that kind of social insurance was the constant threat of inflation. In the fifties, the Eisenhower administration's fiscal policies for the most part had kept the lid on prices by aiming for and achieving a relatively modest growth rate. But well suited as these policies may have been to our mature, inflation-prone economy, they did not go unchallenged. In the campaign of 1960, in fact, John F. Kennedy sharply attacked the moderate policies of the Eisenhower era. Kennedy asked for a chance to get the United States moving again, and a majority of the American voters responded positively to his evocation of the renewal theme.

Presidents John F. Kennedy and Lyndon B. Johnson both felt that America—like Fat Fred—had gone dead in the water in the fifties. Eisenhower, in their view, had not provided vigorous leadership in dealing with the demands of blacks for new opportunities or the needs of millions of other Americans for new social welfare measures. They adopted a larger vision of the federal government's role both at home and abroad. Kennedy proclaimed a New Frontier and peopled his administration with young, dynamic leaders who were commissioned to energize the bureaucracies they headed. After Kennedy's tragic assassination, President Johnson pushed through the Kennedy programs and then set forth his own progressive vision of the Great Society.

Much was accomplished in Washington, D.C., during these busy years. In addition to passing the landmark civil rights measures of 1964 and 1965, Congress gave the federal government a variety of new and difficult tasks to perform. To deal with urban blight, to jack up the economies of depressed regions, to improve our schools and means of transportation, to provide medical care for the poor and elderly, to sustain the arts and humanities—to do all of that the United States had to build a great new structure of triocracies. By the late sixties that system was fully charged and its activities were producing sympathetic resonations throughout America's new economic and political institutions.

As a result of these initiatives, both defense and non-defense expenditures increased sharply and the system's inflationary tendencies were stimulated. By 1968 the federal deficit—due in large part to the war in Vietnam—was up to about $25 billion (compared with $3.1 billion in 1950 and a surplus of $.3 billion in 1960). The deficit supercharged an economy already operating near full capacity, increasing again the country's troublesome rate of inflation. By that time many Americans had begun to wonder whether their country could indeed afford both guns and butter without crippling its new economic system.

By 1968 it was becoming clear that neither hyperactivity nor a placid float would do for a powerful, wealthy, but distinctly middle-aged nation. The dangers of inaction had become evident in the area of civil rights in the fifties and even more so in the sixties. Then, there was a rush of legislation favoring minority rights. Encouraged from one side by the promise of the new laws but hemmed in on the other side by powerful institutions which were slow to respond to the civil rights movement, urban blacks took out their rage in the riots of 1967 and 1968. Spasmodic, a-ideological, and highly emotional, the riots set a pattern that would soon threaten to become the characteristic form of protest against the new American system and the policies adopted by its major institutions. The New Left would fit this mold exactly. But to understand the context in which the New Left movement arose, we must look in the next chapter at the broad outlines of the foreign policy of America at middle age.

7

DEFENDING THE FRONTIERS
OF THE AMERICAN EMPIRE

The players in the National Football League are very big, very fast, and marvelously skilled at doing a small number of things. So specialized are the players, in fact, that the coaches and owners must watch with great care when any changes are made in the rules. Even a minor adjustment can make it difficult for some of their best players to do as well as they have in the past. Of course some players and some teams avoid obsolescence better than others, and in recent years the best of all at adapting to the changing conditions of the game have been the Dallas Cowboys. Whatever the reason—and it probably has something to do with the team's coach, Tom Landry—the Cowboys are always slightly ahead of the pack, making the best possible use of the players they have.

Judged by these same standards, the men and institutions directing U.S. foreign policy in the present century have more resembled the Chicago Bears than they have the Cowboys. The Bears are slow to change. They always seem to be about five years behind the Cowboys. They normally lose. I don't mean to be too harsh in this evaluation. After all, the United States has survived (as have the Bears) a series of revolutionary transformations in this century, and Americans have done so in a manner that at times deserved praise. But throughout, our country has been fighting a long-term holding action—and gradually we have been forced to give ground, sometimes, like the Bears, in rather substantial chunks. We have found it particularly difficult to understand why this should be the case, why a nation as powerful as the United States apparently should be locked in a loser's position, fighting always to preserve the status quo. Surely this is a subject that calls for some discussion.

At the beginning of the twentieth century there was no reason to believe that this would be our fate. Then, the United States was just emerging as the world's leading industrial power. No longer would Americans have to depend on capital from abroad. We were still short of labor and were attracting to this nation millions of southern and eastern European immigrants. They were helping build up the enormously productive industrial system which complemented America's efficient agriculture. Soon, however, immigrants would no longer be needed, and by that time too the United States would be wealthy enough to send its own capital abroad in search of investments. The nation was also ready to flex its muscles, to send its fleet and marines overseas, along with American dollars.

We were not of course the first nation to climb to the top of the economic mountain and contemplate a new and more powerful role in world affairs. In the three centuries since the first American colonies had been settled, one nation after another had gone through this experience and had for a time played a dominant role in global politics. Americans had no reason to believe that they would be deprived of their turn to share in all the kingdoms of the world.

Indeed, in the years prior to the First World War, the United States appeared to be following closely a script based on the past three centuries of Western history. In the Caribbean, we used our navy and army to acquire new territory. We began to intrude rather often in the affairs of other nations both great and small. In the Far East, we established new outposts and pressed our commercial interests with greater vigor. In dealing with Europe we were more hesitant to intrude, but once the First World War began, the United States assumed an economic and later a military position commensurate with its industrial might.

The period between 1896 and 1917 was, indeed, the golden age of America's commercial empire. Much of the world was relatively open to penetration by our businessmen. The major European powers were preoccupied with their own long-standing conflicts at home and abroad. They were hesitant to challenge the United States on the turf it now called its own—in Latin America, for example. There to the south the essential elements of the U.S. domain could be seen most clearly. Economic interests. Diplomatic pressures. Military power. The combination varied from country to country, from year to year. Our empire's boundaries were still mushy. But the empire was certainly there, symbolized by the Panama Canal, which served our commerce and strategy equally well. It also conveniently measured America's dominance of the Caribbean.

The First World War briefly threw open even more markets in Latin America and elsewhere to attentive U.S. businesses, but that great conflict also started a series of social and political upheavals that would gradually erode America's business empire. Some countries would be isolated entirely from capitalistic penetration; others would impose tight national controls on commercial relations. The Russian Revolution launched this process of change. Right-wing movements in the interwar years (in fascist Germany and Italy, for example) had a similar, although less permanent impact on our business relations abroad. Whether these developments were ideologically inspired from the right or the left, they resulted in

Europe and elsewhere in the sort of barriers that made American economic relations more tenuous than they had been before World War I.

As a result, the United States was unable to enjoy the fruits of economic ascendency in the same way that other nations had. In effect the rules of the game had begun to change just as America came to world power. Since that time we have been struggling to prevent additional upheavals that would threaten our economic, military, and diplomatic ties. We have frequently been successful. But even then we have not been able to turn back the clock, to acquire for instance an overall position comparable to the one the United States had achieved before the end of the First World War. New movements on the left and right have repeatedly threatened our interests. That is why the spirit of containment has characterized American policy since World War I. The central aim of our diplomacy has been to contain forces of change that endanger our advantages on the outposts of the American empire.

In Latin America following the First World War, the United States gradually and hesitantly backed away from the aggressive stance taken in the prewar years. The belligerent policies associated with Theodore Roosevelt were quietly repudiated. Eventually we even removed the marines who had been sent into countries such as Nicaragua to ensure that policies we approved would be followed. The United States awkwardly made its peace with the Mexican Revolution, leaving our giant oil companies to look for more friendly sources of crude oil to exploit. The companies grumbled, but the State Department persisted. Rather than assert our strength directly in the tradition of T.R., the United States attempted to work out regional accords that would achieve some of the same ends. Out of this effort came U.S. support for a series of pan-American conferences which wove a delicate web of agreements specifying what one country could do to another in this hemisphere. In the 1930s we became Good Neighbors (which suggests quite accurately that we were something less than that before). But of course we kept the Panama Canal and hung onto the naval bases we had acquired at the turn of the century. We were changing the form more than the substance of our commercial empire in Latin America.

In Asia during the interwar years, the United States found it more difficult to use international agreements to protect the eastern reaches of our realm. Here, unlike Latin America, a major power emerged to challenge the United States. Japan's rise to world power had begun before World War I, had accelerated during that great conflict, and had begun to present in the 1920s and 1930s a major threat to U.S. interests. We attempted in a series of naval conferences to bring Japanese expansionism under control. By the late thirties, however, that policy was clearly bankrupt. Neither the form nor the substance of restraint existed, even though we still clung to our outposts in the Far East and attempted to exact concessions from the Japanese as we slowly gave way before their aggressive expansion.

In Europe, where before the First World War we had acquired the weakest foothold and where after the peace conference we did the least to maintain our position, the United States lost ground more quickly. Unstable conditions within and between the powers, great and small, left Europe vulnerable to revolutions from the left and right. Whether the changes took the form of fascism, as they did in Germany and Italy, or communism, as they had in Russia, the outcomes were unfavorable for America's politico-economic interests. In the thirties in particular, when the worldwide depression encouraged the growth of economic nationalism, the United States found more and more countries bringing their trade under control in ways that worked to America's disadvantage. To those who were critical of U.S. isolationism in the thirties, it seemed that the United States was only getting what it deserved for its disregard of European affairs in the aftermath of the First World War. Even to those who were less idealistic, it should have been apparent that the United States was not doing a particularly good job of understanding and responding to the changes taking place in that part of the world.

In the 1940s—the watershed decade for our domestic institutions—America's commercial empire was also transformed. Blended with the customary policies of promoting business ties and resisting revolutionary change was a powerful new concern for America's national security. For the first time in well over a century, the continental United States was no longer secure from a direct and potentially devastating attack. The same sorts of scientific and technological advances that were crucial to our agricultural revolution and industrial productivity had also yielded an atomic bomb and long-range aircraft and rockets that made the United States vulnerable. The American people first began to sense this change during the war. Long before the German surrender, in fact, our political leaders had clearly signaled that the United States would be more heavily committed to our friends and trading partners around the world than it had been in the 1930s. So far as possible, we would seek our goals through international organization and understanding. But with America no longer safe beyond its ocean barriers, there was more consideration of how our military power should be used to protect our interests abroad.

As Russia's intentions became clearer and more threatening, U.S. political and military leaders stitched together the traditional policy of the commercial empire and the new strategy of anticommunism. The United States reacted strongly when Russia consolidated its position in Eastern Europe, walling off Poland, Rumania, Bulgaria, Hungary, Yugoslavia, and East Germany from the dominant capitalist power in the West. With Turkey and Greece threatened by a similar fate, and both France and Italy unstable enough to arouse serious doubts about their political future, the United States in the late forties committed its power and wealth to an effort to shore up these nations and to keep them outside the communist bloc. In 1948 the extent of that commitment increased sharply after Czechoslovakia fell to a communist coup.

The United States recast its empire. Boundaries that had been vague and flexible were now rendered precise and firm. Alliances spelled out our commitments. Military bases around the world pushed American power into many countries with which we did not have and probably never would have extensive economic ties. Never mind. Our objective was to keep those nations on our side of the line that divided the globe—as we perceived it—between the communist and noncommunist societies. There was fear on our side that the United States might be defeated piecemeal if we allowed one country after another to slip across that line. Where would it end? Would the United States be left completely isolated, cut off from the world's trade and threatened by the same sort of devastation that had taken place in Europe during World War II? These questions, framed as part of our anticommunist ideology, frequently made it difficult for Americans to distinguish between the important and the less important outposts of their empire. The containment of change thus became a more deadly and universal concern after 1945.

It would be unnecessary to cover these familiar developments at such length had not the critics of our foreign policy caused so much misunderstanding in recent years. Many of them have charged U.S. leaders with causing the Cold War. They have pointed to the policies of the American empire as proof that an aggressive U.S. stance drove the Russians into a corner and left them no alternative but to behave as they did. In my view, however, we should credit the Russians (whose archives we cannot examine) with being at least as perceptive about their long-run interests as was the United States (whose archives have now been thoroughly studied by scholars). The Russians had much to gain in Eastern Europe. They had the power to get what they wanted and they took the opportunity provided by Germany's collapse. The United States, which was dedicated to preserving as much as it could of its own position in Europe, found that it could not contain the forces of change without putting its money and military power on the line. When the United States did this, it began to transform the commercial empire into a much more formidable entity, scattering air bases, naval stations, and army divisions along its overseas frontiers. We now resisted change more forcefully than before, and many Americans began to see every new development abroad as originating somehow in Moscow.

Even in Asia, where the links between Russia and indigenous communist forces were relatively slight, Americans perceived a monolithic Red Wave spreading over the continent. We tried for years to prevent the Chinese Communists from driving out the corrupt regime we supported, but in 1949 the Communists completed their conquest of the mainland. When in 1950 the Korean War erupted, the United States put its armed forces, as well as its economic support, into the effort to prevent further losses in the Far East.

By that time, of course, the United States was already heavily involved in the defense of Western Europe. The North Atlantic Treaty Organization was the first of a series of military alliances that by 1954 clearly defined the frontiers of the American empire. Like the treaties of the 1920s, these understandings generalized the American interests, spreading responsibility among a number of participating countries; unlike those earlier agreements, however, the post–World War II pacts specifically called for the direct involvement of American military power. Not till the 1960s would the United States discover just how dangerous and expensive that involvement could be.

Under ideal circumstances, the new system of defenses,

the treaties, and U.S. foreign aid payments could have done nothing more than preserve the status quo. The policies were all designed to achieve that end, to prevent change. But Americans were slow to realize that this was the main thrust of their own foreign policy and that this was what they were paying billions of dollars and many lives to achieve. Middle age sneaks up on you like that. In the 1940s it still seemed almost un-American to be that dedicated merely to keeping things as they were. Growth had always been an important part of our national culture. But now we were playing for a tie. By talking about the defense of the free world, we made the policy more palatable, even though that made it hard to explain why there were so many military governments and dictatorships on our side. Moreover, that theme—the defense of freedom—made it tempting to look for an expansion of freedom through a more aggressive posture than the U.S. military-economic policies were designed to achieve.

In the fifties, even President Eisenhower briefly gave in to that temptation. He allowed his supporters to proclaim that our aim was to roll back the forces of communism, "liberating the captive peoples" of Eastern Europe. Talk like this made good news in America's ethnic communities. The Poles, Czechs, Rumanians, Lithuanians, Latvians, and Estonians who had come to the United States but remained concerned about their homelands were encouraged to believe that the United States might now do something forceful to return those nations to their prewar forms of government. Many Hungarian-Americans shared this hope.

In 1956 when the Hungarian people revolted against their government, however, the United States did nothing to support the uprising. As Russian tanks crushed the revolution, the main outlines of American foreign policy were etched in the headlines of our newspapers. Containment was just that. The United States was using its power in an effort to preserve unchanged the far-flung outposts of its empire. There actually never had been and probably never would be any aggressive effort to expand those frontiers.

Such an effort would have been far beyond the limits of American military power to achieve. As president, Eisenhower was no more likely to overextend our military establishment than he had been as supreme commander in World War II. Indeed, the central theme of Eisenhower's presidency was his effort to balance with care our resources and the country's goals. In foreign as in domestic policy, Eisenhower looked upon those resources as relatively inflexible. Hence he tailored the goals of our national government to fit those means— doing the kind of cautious political accounting that befitted America at middle age. As a result, the nation won a few limited victories, lost a few encounters of the same sort, but avoided throughout a major international confrontation. In the 1950s, some Americans were critical of this restrained approach to foreign policy. After the problems of the sixties and seventies, however, the Eisenhower stance began to look more appealing.

It was, after all, no small achievement to dampen the pressures making for military involvement on America's far-reaching frontiers. For one thing, the United States had to contend with the powerful forces unleashed by the breakdown of the old colonial empires in Asia and Africa. There was virtually nothing the United States could do, despite all of its military power, to shore up the positions of its NATO allies in the Third World. One after another, they gave way to the demands of the colonies for independence. But more often than not, these demands had to be won amidst violence that left the former colonies hostile to the West and to its leading power, the United States. Frequently, too, the leaders of the revolutionary movements were Socialists or Communists. They correctly perceived that the United States was the friendly supporter of the governments that long had kept their countries in subjection and were quick to point out that American power was being used to prevent, not to promote, change. They were correct. What they forgot, however, was that the United States had in the Second World War fought against changes from the right with even greater vigor and with success. America was the enemy of threatening developments from any quarter, but after 1945, most of these came from the left.

In the 1950s, after the truce in Korea, the United States managed for a few years to avoid direct involvement in the military struggles generated by these revolutions. The closest we came was one episode in Central America and one in the Mideast. In Guatemala, the U.S. Central Intelligence Agency conducted an undercover operation that resulted in the overthrow of the government of President Jacobo Arbenz Guzmán. In Lebanon, American power was exerted more directly, in the tradition of our prewar Latin American policy, with the Marine Corps landing to protect a U.S.–supported regime. In neither case, however, did the United States become involved in a protracted military campaign; in both cases, the efforts were characterized by a high level of hypocrisy and low costs in men and arms. This was a balance that most Americans could support, if only because they wanted so desperately to go on believing that their country was still the friend of freedom around the world.

But in the 1960s that faith was shaken when more ambitious presidents abandoned the restrained policies that had characterized Eisenhower's administrations. John F. Kennedy and Lyndon B. Johnson did not change in any dramatic fashion the basic goals of the nation's foreign policy. It is unlikely that any president could have done that in the past quarter of a century or will be able to in the foreseeable future. We have little choice but to continue fighting a holding operation on the frontiers of America's empire, protecting our friends and trading partners, whether they add to or subtract from the rights of man, and defending our national security by maintaining our forces and base system. But under Kennedy and Johnson, the United States became much more aggressive in its efforts to achieve those goals. We experimented with new means of preserving a world friendly to America's interests.

Not all of these new policies involved military force. Not all of them were dangerous or deserving of our criticism. The Peace Corps was, for instance, a laudable effort to help other countries. Perhaps the only unfortunate effect of the Peace Corps was that it reinforced the basic American desire to see our international relations in a far more favorable light than most of the rest of the world thought was reasonable. In that sense the Peace Corps helped preserve the gap that has developed between our self-image and our international public image. Still, who would reject a policy as farsighted as the Peace Corps on these grounds alone?

Unfortunately, the Marine Corps played a more decisive role in America's relations abroad than did the Peace Corps in the sixties. As our country's leaders took a more expansive view of America's resources, they involved the United States in two disastrous international adventures. One was the ill-planned Bay of Pigs invasion of Cuba in 1961. This humiliating defeat, which weakened our position throughout Latin America, revealed quite clearly the problems U.S. leaders were having in understanding the revolutionary process in other countries. Our attempt to turn back the clock in Cuba was ill-conceived in political as well as military terms. Even if the invasion had succeeded temporarily, the United States would have lost out eventually in that country—as it did in Vietnam. The Vietnamese War was a far more costly struggle, and the country continues today to pay a price for that serious blunder. When the dust of the sixties finally settles for good, historians are likely to conclude that it was the most debilitating episode in the nation's entire history, more expensive in its own special way than World Wars I and II combined.

The U.S. entanglement in Southeast Asia had actually begun long before John Kennedy took office in 1961. But until that time, the United States had been satisfied to "arrange" for the Vietnamese to have leaders friendly to our country, to bankroll military operations against the revolutionary forces, to provide the guns that these dollars could buy for the U.S.– trained armed forces deployed by the leaders we had selected. This was hardly an exercise in democracy or freedom, but it was nonetheless restrained by the standards set a few years later.

President Kennedy gradually increased the U.S. commitment, and his successor put even more troops and guns on the line in a futile attempt to stabilize this frontier of the American empire. If the new effort had succeeded quickly— even at achieving a stalemate, à la Korea—there is little reason to believe that the American public would have been particularly concerned. The repressive features of the regimes we supported would have aroused no more discontent than Americans are expressing today about the similarly repressive governments we are backing around the world. Be honest. How much do you get exercised about the South Korean government today?

But in Vietnam, American wealth and military power failed to contain the forces of change. The United States bought time, as it had earlier in Greece and Iran. In Vietnam, however, the time was shorter and the price far higher— higher even than it had been in Western Europe in the late forties. The first small step was to increase the number of military advisers, then the special forces, then the financial aid, then the military advisers and arms again. When President Kennedy was assassinated, there were over sixteen thousand troops committed to the struggle; three years later, President Johnson had put more than three hundred and fifty thousand troops into a war that had destroyed vast parts of the country we were ostensibly saving for the free world.

The cost—in men, in wealth, in domestic discord—eventually broke the back of America's war effort. The United States mounted a fierce air war against North Vietnam. Our ground forces in ever increasing numbers took over the major combat role in South Vietnam. By the end of 1966 the United States had lost well over six thousand men, and had nothing to show for these losses except a deeper, more devastating involvement in a war that American firepower apparently could never end. When Lyndon Johnson finally left office, the country was spending about half a billion dollars a week to support its ill-fated military campaign. Over thirty thousand Americans were dead or missing in action and 183,000 had been wounded in the Vietnamese War.

These losses and the other costs of war might have been acceptable had we been defending one of the Western democracies from foreign aggression. But in Southeast Asia we were fighting to prop up a corrupt government which ruled a land in which we had never had a significant economic or political stake. To justify the war you had to believe that all of the foreign frontiers of our empire were equally important to U.S. security. Or that once we lost our foothold in Vietnam a long-run process of change would inevitably bring down the governments of all the contiguous countries. Or that a communist victory would irreparably damage U.S. prestige, as had clearly not been the case after the Communists won control of mainland China in 1949. None of these arguments have much intellectual appeal.

In the seventies the American public gradually began to see this, recognizing at last the profound imbalance between what we were giving up and what we hoped to gain. But long before that happened a smaller number of young people had started to express their outrage at Johnson's (and then Nixon's) war. The New Left movement of these years began as an effort to seek reform in the United States through regular political channels. At each turn, however, the movement's leaders ran into the icy hard surface of the country's new political and economic institutions. Whether they confronted the presidents of universities, the spokesmen for corporations, or elected political leaders, they were fended off and denied what they thought was a fair hearing for their ideas. Initially most of the ideas were liberal and relatively moderate. Blacks, they thought, should be allowed to vote and even run for office. The war in Southeast Asia, they said, was an unwarranted imperialistic effort to thwart a nationalist movement. They argued too that women deserved equal access to responsible positions that had long been denied to them solely on the basis of their sex.

When responsible authorities ignored these ideas and the war effort was stepped up, the New Left movement became increasingly radical. Now its leaders attacked the very basis of the country's most powerful institutions. Capitalism itself became the enemy, as did the universities that did research for the military, the government that conducted the war, the political parties that sustained a system the leaders of the New Left now portrayed as rotten to its core. Even American culture was, they decided, repressive. All of this had to be thrown out and replaced by a new style of society.

Lacking a stable ideology, the New Left lashed out at the entire American system, focusing now on one issue, now on another. Peaceful methods gave way to forceful resistance. Reason gave way to emotion. Like a hurricane over open sea, the New Left gathered force in the late 1960s when the fighting in Vietnam reached its peak. By the end of the decade, the movement had drawn into its ranks many Americans who were neither young nor radical. They too had begun to mistrust their own government. They too wanted America to leave Vietnam to the Vietnamese. They too recognized that the United States had to find some better way to achieve its objectives in Asia and the rest of the world. As their opposition gradually filtered through to Congress, the Nixon administration was forced at last to negotiate a cease-fire and then to begin peace talks.

By then, however, the New Left was falling apart. Like an insect that stings its enemy and then dies, the movement was collapsing just as its major goal was achieved. It died out almost as quickly as the urban riots. Both movements were brief but fierce; both left behind a residue of bitter feeling and doubt. That, it would appear, was to be the characteristic pattern of political resistance to the new American system of powerful, well-organized, deeply entrenched institutions. Liberalism had lost its appeal. Americans would either work through their interest groups inside the system, or they would mount fierce frontal attacks (the next one from the right) to gain some single, immediate objective. If our political leaders allowed either our domestic or foreign policies to get out of hand, they could expect to provoke just this sort of emotional all-out attack.

In the sixties, the policy on Vietnam inspired such an uprising and for a time left the country sharply divided and in doubt. All that could be certain was that our leaders had blundered seriously. The United States at middle age needed a better sense of priorities as to when and where and why it would exercise its great power. But before those priorities could be established, a new crisis arose at home. It was, all in all, a difficult time to be an American.

8

THE THIRD PHASE

In the 1970s Jack Nicholson starred in several outstanding movies, winning an Oscar for his performance in *One Flew Over the Cuckoo's Nest*. His roles were varied. In *Five Easy Pieces*, he played a concert pianist gone bad; in *The Last Detail*, he was a career sailor; in *Chinatown*, a detective. Whatever his occupation, however, the character Nicholson portrayed in all of these films had one outstanding characteristic. He always lost. He was often clever and sometimes vicious—but he always lost. As was most evident in *Carnal Knowledge* (1971), Nicholson was the symbol of sardonic impotence, an appropriate symbol for America in the seventies.

Gail Sheehy's best-seller, *Passages*, explained that feelings of impotence are a common problem in the middle-aged man. They can be caused by real physical difficulties. Most often, however, they are a product of fear and anxiety. The middle-aged man who becomes for whatever reason concerned about his sexual prowess worries himself into impotence. Rather than accepting—indeed, capitalizing on—his maturity, he psychs himself into "a humiliating failure." Loss of confidence in this case breeds a loss of ability. In America during the seventies there was a great deal of fear and anxiety, feelings

125

that were linked to a growing sense of impotence about America and about some of its most important public and private institutions.

II

At the very beginning of the decade, things seemed to get better. It appeared for a time that the nation was about to regain the sort of peace and prosperity that had characterized the fifties. The parallels were exciting to those who looked back to the Eisenhower era with longing. In the White House there was a Republican leader who had repeatedly proclaimed his determination to bring the country's swollen budget deficits under control. The excesses of the sixties had left the United States, as President Nixon explained in June 1970, with deficits totaling $57 billion. (Keep this figure in mind.) Now it was time to travel "the road of responsibility." On that highway, the policy would be "to cut down the sharp rise in Federal spending and to restrain the economy firmly and steadily." This was what Eisenhower had done about the inflationary spiral caused by the Korean War. Nixon seemed to be guided by the same principles. He used the veto to defeat inflationary spending measures. He called on business and labor leaders to display restraint about prices and wage hikes. He chopped $6 billion out of the budgets for defense and space exploration.

Crucial to the Eisenhower cuts had been a quick end to the hostilities in Korea, and Nixon made it clear that he was bent on achieving the same sort of settlement in Vietnam. He was bringing home American troops. He was paring down defense spending. He was guiding the nation through a "transition from a wartime economy to a peacetime economy." Seldom had the intertwining of domestic and foreign policy been made so clear as it was in this early phase of the Nixon administration.

Along with the effort to scale down our involvement in

Vietnam came a radical departure in our policy toward Communist China. As part of his effort "to build a lasting peace in the world," President Nixon sent his assistant for national security affairs to discuss normalization of relations with China's leaders. The President himself accepted an invitation to visit China in 1972. The Nixon initiative resulted in the establishment of full diplomatic relations between the two nations, and, incidentally, helped many Americans recognize for the first time that the communist nations of the world were not a monolithic Red Bloc controlled from Moscow. Nixon's innovative policy on this front was one of the most outstanding accomplishments of his presidency.

In dealing with Southeast Asia, however, Nixon was less innovative, less honest, and far less successful. He began to remove America's ground forces and to turn this part of the war over to the South Vietnamese. But at the same time he tried to drive the war to a favorable conclusion with a massive exercise of air power. The new approach saved the lives of American soldiers. The last of the ground forces pulled out of Vietnam in 1972. But by that time we had spread the war into Cambodia and launched full-scale attacks on North Vietnam. The large-scale bombing of Cambodia—conducted in secret against the territory of a neutral country—was especially difficult for the American people to understand or accept. They wanted out and their protests finally forced the administration to give up its futile air campaign.

The result was a face-saving agreement that at last left the ineffective South Vietnamese government to fend for itself. Fifteen months later the government collapsed, and a renewed communist offensive swept into the capital city of Saigon (April 1975). Instead of a Korean-type stalemate, the outcome was a paralyzing defeat. We had invested billions of dollars, had sacrificed 58,000 American lives, had endured years of internal strife, only to see Saigon renamed Ho Chi Minh City. Neither U.S. ground forces nor U.S. air power

had been able to prevent that outcome, and the American
people emerged from this experience with an understandable
anxiety about what their expensive military establishment
actually could do.

The expenditures were substantial and that too bred
concern at home. Despite his talk about a transition from a
war to a peace economy, Nixon did not reduce defense
spending significantly. Between 1970 and 1974, actual outlays
for the military fell less than a billion dollars. Determined to
achieve a particular kind of settlement, the U.S. poured additional dollars down the Vietnamese rathole. Instead of fueling
an economic recovery as they had in the forties, the wartime
outlays of the seventies created new inflationary pressures in
an already overheated economy. America's modern political
and economic institutions all leaned toward inflation. When
fiscal policy added a push in that direction, the system quickly
reacted to the stimulus by going into an inflationary spiral.
By the time Nixon left office, the United States was experiencing double-digit inflation.

The total deficit in the years 1970–1974 actually eclipsed
the figures from the entire decade of the sixties ($58.7 billion
vs. $57 billion, the figure you were told to remember), and
for this the Republican administration bears only partial responsibility. Between 1970 and 1974, federal spending that
was unrelated to defense increased by more than $70 billion;
payments to individuals (especially for social security and for
Medicare and Medicaid) went up by over $50 billion, and aid
to state and local governments increased by almost $20
billion. Powerful triocracies were exerting strong pressures
to increase expenditures, just when our middle-aged economy
most needed restraint. Congress yielded to these demands,
and the results included mounting deficits and an inflation
so severe that it began in the seventies to twist the economy
out of shape. The institutions that were supposed to stabilize
our national economy were not doing their job, and the

American people had good cause to criticize their political leaders for what was happening.

The crucial years were 1973–1974, when the government's income turned up sharply but outlays were still allowed to go up, keeping the country in a deficit position. At that important juncture, the Nixon administration was unable to provide the country with the forceful leadership that might have put brakes on the economy. Just when their guidance was most needed, the chief executive and the top officers in his administration were busy elsewhere, preoccupied with the effort to conceal their own corruption.

By the spring of 1973, the public phase of the most debilitating series of scandals ever to touch the presidency was beginning to unfold. Struggling unsuccessfully to hide his own illegal actions, the president was forced in 1973 to give ground. A special prosecutor was appointed to investigate the administration's role in an unsuccessful effort to burglarize the Washington campaign headquarters of the Democratic party; the prosecutor was also charged with probing the administration's attempts to cover up that illegal activity. Congress held its own investigation and started hearings in May 1973. What emerged was a disheartening picture of weak men and weakened public institutions.

Just as the fury over the Watergate scandal was starting, Vice President Spiro T. Agnew suddenly resigned from office. The vice president of the United States pleaded no contest to charges that he had received bribes from Maryland contractors. Even after he had begun to serve in the nation's second highest political office, Agnew had continued to receive his cash payments in a white, unmarked envelope.

Agnew's disgrace was damaging to an administration that had preached at length about the need for law and order, but the months that followed brought even worse news for those who had hoped that Richard Nixon would be the strong national leader America needed in the seventies. As the investigations pressed home, the administration scurried from one defensive position to another. Loyal supporters were thrown to the courts. Officials who refused to yield to Nixon's demands were dismissed. The turnover rate in the executive branch of our government was astonishing. Between January 1973 and the fall of 1974, for example, four different men held the post of attorney general of the United States. All to no avail. The dismissals and denials failed. Nixon too was forced to resign, on August 9, 1974.

It would be nice if I could say that the nation's problems melted like lemon drops when Nixon boarded the Spirit of '76 and flew to California, but that was not the case. His successor, Gerald Ford, was honest but ineffective. He launched his short stay in the White House by mounting a weak and unsuccessful campaign against inflation. Even if he had not formally pardoned Nixon in August 1974 and thus undercut his political support, Ford would probably have been unable to bring under control the strong interests pressing hard for heavier federal outlays. Congress responded with enthusiasm to those pressures. As a result, the economy experienced stagflation. Gross national product was down in these recession years; prices and unemployment were up. In 1975 the federal deficit soared to over $45 billion. The next year it was more than $66 billion (see how important it was to remember that figure for the sixties!). Inconsistent, inept, and corrupt leaders were creating deficits that the country's modern system of political economy simply could not tolerate over the long haul. A middle-aged society deserved and certainly needed better hands than these on the helm.

To solve these enormous national problems the voters turned in 1976 to a little-known politician from Georgia, Jimmy Carter. Insiders had failed them. The people looked to a new type of man, one who would make up in sincerity and personal stature what he lacked in national and international experience. But the results were disappointing. Carter was no more effective then Gerald Ford, and Congress casually thwarted his best efforts. That happened in the first months of his administration, when a president usually has about as much leverage against Congress as he ever will have. In the backwash of Vietnam and Watergate, however, the legislature was bent on regaining power from what some observers had begun to refer to as the Imperial Presidency. In that spirit, Congress ignored Carter's plans to deal with the energy problem created by the international oil cartel, the Organization of Petroleum Exporting Countries (OPEC). Likewise, the president's idealistic proposals to reorganize the federal bureaucracy were trampled in a rush to pass special interest legislation. The country's triocracies were not interested in suicide. Instead, they asked for and got new funds, and the resulting deficits gave another jolt to the country's already high rate of inflation. The dollar grew weaker abroad, as did America's prestige. At home, even Carter, an honest man, turned out to have some questionable friends—and an embarrassing brother—who raised doubts about the integrity as well as the efficacy of the administration. With the ship of state settling in the water, Carter in desperation shook up his cabinet in 1979, replacing many of his most important advisers. By this time instability of leadership had become a hallmark of the seventies, and the voters got into this spirit in 1980, when they rejected Carter's reelection bid by an impressive margin.

If Americans felt powerless by that time, their last three presidents had given them plenty of reasons to lose their confidence. Taxes were high. The economy was too fragile. Inflation was steadily cutting into the purchasing power of the dollar. Our economic policies seemed muddled and the future promised more problems of the same sort. In the new American system, responsibility for these matters rested with the president. Even though he did not have the authority to control unilaterally the government's monetary or fiscal policies, the president was the executive officer to whom the public looked when our economic performance fell short of their expectations. During the seventies neither Republican nor Democratic presidents had been able to provide the kind of leadership that the new system needed. They had in fact sadly diminished the office of the presidency itself by corruption and weakness.

III

Nor could Americans look to Congress for the leadership the White House failed to provide. The legislature during this decade had compiled a regrettable record. Even when the presidents attempted to bring spending under control, Congress pressed for more of the outlays that would satisfy the interest groups and the folks back home. Triocracy unrestrained was an inherently expansive system. It was also Congress that bore primary responsibility for gradually tipping the balance of federal expenditures away from defense and toward transfer payments to individuals. These latter payments were relatively inflexible. Federal expenditures for welfare and related programs were more difficult to control than defense spending; outlays for social programs could not be delayed, and recipients responded to proposed cutbacks with those prompt and supercharged protests that make a legislator quiver with concern about his reelection. While there was much to be said for spending to protect human resources rather than to destroy them, the new emphasis in the federal budget made it ever more difficult to use fiscal policy to control the national economy. For that Congress bore heavy responsibility, just as it did for the nation's inflation-generating deficits. In the seventies America's triocratic polity failed to fill the gaps in our national leadership left by the country's presidents.

Congress actually matched the White House for corruption. Sandwiched between some run-of-the-mill kickback and bribery scandals, there was an extensive investigation of South Korean influence on the House of Representatives. The South Korean front man in Washington had lavished entertainment and ample funds on selected congressmen, and so serious were the charges in this case that the House of Representatives actually voted to reprimand three of its members. Normally congressional self-policing produces strong sanctions about as often as do local law enforcement investigations of police brutality. None of us really expects self-policing to work. We tolerate these symbolic gestures because we don't really care very much about the results. So we can assume that when the House went so far as to vote in favor of formal reprimands, a number of very serious offenses had been committed—the sort of thing that would have sent private citizens to prison for a few years.

When state and federal courts became involved in such affairs that was exactly what they did with selected congressmen. Instead of light wrist-slapping, a federal court in Michigan sentenced Congressman Charles C. Diggs, Jr., to a three-year prison term for mail fraud and other assorted crimes. In Pennsylvania, Congressman Daniel J. Flood crowned his thirty-one-year career of public service by pleading guilty to charges that he had accepted illegal campaign contributions. By pleading guilty and resigning his office, he managed to stay out of prison, but the judge nevertheless placed Flood, who was seventy-six and ill, on a year's probation. Most telling of all were the Abscam investigations. Thanks to the marvel of modern technology, the American public could see and hear the videotaped record of Congressman Michael O. Myers taking a bribe and explaining how the federal legislature worked: "It's a big pie down in Washington. Each member's sent there to bring a piece of that pie back home. And if you go down there and you don't—you came back without milkin' it after a few terms . . . you don't go . . . back." Pictures of an elected official eagerly stuffing large wads of bribe money in his pockets stuck in the mind, leaving the public to wonder whether the rotten apples outnumbered the good ones in the barrel on Capitol Hill.

Abscam was an appropriate bookend for a decade that had produced a new low-water mark for American political leadership at the federal level. If one sifts through the pages of U.S. history, it is hard to find a decade that was worse than this one. The 1920s and the Harding scandals only come in third. The 1870s stand out as a solid contestant for second place. But none can rival the 1970s. Then, so poor were the records of the executive and legislative branches of our government that they actually made a rather mediocre judiciary—even the Supreme Court's reputation was sagging—look relatively good. If by the end of the decade many Americans were extremely anxious about the future of their middle-aged society, much of their anxiety could be traced to the poor quality of our national leadership.

IV

The problem was not just one of personal corruption; many of our most important public institutions were performing in questionable ways. The Watergate mire spilled over onto the Central Intelligence Agency. This creature of our post-1945 concern for national security had for many years unsettled liberals who were nervous about what the highly secret organization was doing. Threats to our civil liberties at home were a particular concern, even though the CIA's charter specifically limited the agency to overseas spying. A report in 1975 on the CIA's activities suggested that these fears were realistic, as did the conviction in 1977 of the former director of the agency for illegally withholding information from Congress.

The Federal Bureau of Investigation suffered a similar

blow in the backwash of Watergate. The Bureau's public image was pitted by a number of serious charges of misconduct. The public learned that longtime FBI director J. Edgar Hoover had for years kept files on many prominent persons, files which were used to protect his bureaucratic fiefdom. (Most of us would call this blackmail if it was done to us.) The Bureau had spied on reform organizations and their leaders, none of whom were associated with any crime other than that of seeking legal political changes in the United States. As these and other charges against the FBI mounted, Americans had good cause to worry about what the law and its enforcement had come to mean in a country some of whose highest law enforcement officers were themselves so worthy of prison terms. It was demoralizing to see pictures of former Attorney General John Mitchell actually entering a prison and even more depressing when you realized that the late director of the FBI should perhaps have spent some time there too.

Our military was also a cause for concern, in spite of the fact that it was the only major institution in our history that had risen to great power without suffering through a long bout with corruption.* Between 1948 and 1968, America's military leaders were entrusted with authority over a significant part of the capital of the wealthiest nation on the earth. They exercised that authority with a commendable degree of probity. But still, in the 1970s there was deep concern about the military, not about its honesty or attachment to duty, but about its efficiency. Could we depend on our army, our navy, our air force? A decade that had begun with the abortive attempt to rescue our prisoners of war from a camp outside Hanoi ended with U.S. helicopters burning after they failed to rescue our hostages in Iran. Between, there was the collapse of the Vietnamese army we had trained and armed. Although

*I promised to tell you this some pages ago. You can stop worrying about it now.

defense spending was allowed to fall behind the rate of inflation, we were still investing over $100 billion a year on national security—and there was reason to wonder how secure we really were. What if the rest of our forces worked as poorly as those helicopters did?

Few such questions had to be asked about the U.S. Postal Service because this branch of the federal government was a source of substantial consensus. So poor and troublesome was the service that Congress had actually given away its control over the U.S. Post Office in 1970. The legislation of that year converted the postal service into an independent agency. Failing to make a public bureaucracy work efficiently, the government in effect "privatized" it. This was a typical American solution to the problems of public administration. For several generations now our political leaders had been bringing various business executives into government service so they could show public bureaucrats how to get things done. Many of the officers of our largest corporations spent a significant part of their careers in public service of one form or another. They were "businesscrats," half public, half private creatures. But howsoever effective they were in the short term, they were apparently unable to work the magic that would over the long run make our public organizations more efficient. In its new form, the Post Office did not appear to be noticeably improved. Service continued to be poor and continued to get more expensive. Ten years after the reform of 1970 it was not apparent that much had been accomplished.

This was not a partisan issue because neither of the two major political parties had much to say about public administration. The Democratic party, since the 1930s the avowed friend of big government, had never really paid much attention to how public institutions could be made more efficient. For that matter neither did the Republican party, which had for years stressed the need to cut back government operations. So obsessed were the parties with the question of how much government to have that they gave little attention to the specifics of how to make the government we did have more effective. This peculiarity persists today, even though the several governments in our middle-aged society are now entrusted with a very large part of our gross national product. The voter who in 1972, 1976, or 1980 wanted to vote for the party most likely to achieve a major, positive breakthrough in improving public sector efficiency would have been unable to cast his ballot. In this sense, both parties looked to the nation's political past, not its administrative future.

Of course the Republican party stressed the need to shift more responsibility (meaning dollars) to state and local authorities, but Americans had grounds at the end of the seventies to be skeptical about the performance of those governments too. In New York, for example, they saw a state government pile up enormous debts while it allowed essential services to lag and industry to flee to other parts of the country. The city of New York was in a virtual state of bankruptcy by the middle of the decade, and New York was not alone in this regard. Other cities and states had similar problems, all of which illustrated the need for improved administrative performance at every level of our political system.

In the latter part of the decade the financial problems of state and local governments were so serious that they sparked a wave of tax revolts. The movement began in California, where the voters handcuffed their state and local governments with a specific upper limit on taxes and hence on public revenue. The discontent spread eastward in the months that followed. Few of the measures adopted were as drastic as California's Proposition 13, but all reflected a deep public hostility toward state and local government.

The tax revolt was the third wave of political protest to erupt since the mid-sixties. Like the urban riots and the New Left, the tax revolt bubbled up from the people without benefit of a stable ideology or unified leadership. All three were highly charged, emotional movements which sought extreme solutions to America's problems. As befitted a bourgeois uprising, the tax revolt's means were peaceful and political (so had the New Left's been—at first). But like the previous protests, it was a distinctly grass-roots movement, which arose outside the normal structure of American party politics. It reflected a broad and growing concern about American public institutions, from the White House down to the city hall. If it was going to survive its middle age, the United States apparently needed less expensive, more effective governments. At least that was what the people were trying to tell their leaders.

V

When previous generations had grown dissatisfied with their government, they had always consoled themselves by admiring the country's private institutions. It was not just Calvin Coolidge who thought business was America's true calling. The yardstick for public performance in twentieth-century America had always been the private entrepreneur and his most formidable creation, the giant business corporation. That was why we sent all of those business leaders to Washington to make things run correctly.

In the seventies, however, Americans began to wonder how effective their corporate combines really were. The major problem, which had really surfaced in the late sixties, was the lack of productivity gains in the private sector. Increases in productivity were crucial to an intensive economy of the sort that characterized the United States in the twentieth century. In the fifties and through the first half of the sixties, America's new economic institutions had logged impressive accomplishments, with increases in productivity averaging 2.5 percent per year through 1966. This was the highest sustained rate of increase in the twentieth century. But from

1966 on, our productivity gains—the crucial measure of our ability to innovate—began to get smaller and smaller. At about the same time expenditures for research and development leveled off and the government's support for science and technology actually began to drop. We were sailing a dangerous course. Inflation was distorting our private and public patterns of investment, choking off the elaborate system of institutions that had fostered our increases in efficiency. By the late seventies the U.S. private sector was actually experiencing declines in productivity.

By then there were other signs of weakness, some symbolic, some real. In 1971, Congress had passed special legislation to rescue the giant Lockheed Corporation from bankruptcy. The excuse had been national defense. The firm was an important defense contractor, and the Defense Department argued that Lockheed's expertise would be lost if the government failed to come to the aid of the company. Those of us who were disturbed by this rationalization for the Lockheed subsidy became even more nervous when Chrysler later turned to the government for help. Now the national defense argument wouldn't really cover the situation. The federal budget was being tapped simply because a bankrupt Chrysler corporation would increase unemployment and presumably further weaken the national economy. Chrysler was in trouble for the same reason that the other U.S. automobile producers were hurting. They had all miscalculated, had continued to float along (remember Fred?) producing large cars when the market was shifting toward the smaller, more fuel-efficient automobiles made by foreign companies. The entire industry suffered as a result of this mistake. America's automobile industry, heretofore one of the nation's most innovative and productive, was now a recipient of welfare payments. This made some Americans very uneasy about the future of their country's private sector.

It was not just the automobile companies that were in

trouble either. The steel industry was lagging far behind its technologically advanced foreign competitors. The steel companies blamed government regulations for their problems. The government thought otherwise. But the entire debate— whatever its outcome—made people nervous about the economy's slow rate of growth and lack of productivity gains. There was reason to speculate whether our new economic institutions, as well as our triocratic governments, were not emphasizing security at the price of the system's ability to innovate.

The near disaster at Three Mile Island also generated some new doubts about the efficiency of one of the country's leading science-based industries. In this case the danger was immediate and physical, just as it was when Douglas Aircraft's DC-10s developed metal fatigue in a crucial part that held the jet engine to the plane. In both cases, public as well as private organizations were involved: the Nuclear Regulatory Commission, which was supposed to ensure the safety of the power plants; and the Federal Aviation Agency, which looked after our commercial airlines. In both instances neither the private companies nor their public watchdogs did a good enough job to satisfy the public.

These events left the country troubled about its new economic institutions. Neither our public nor our private organizations seemed to be functioning very well any more. Other countries were faring better in the seventies. Increasingly, Americans began to look overseas and to compare their large-scale, modern organizations with those of other nations. Like a runner who is tightening up on the last lap, the United States at middle age was beginning to glance nervously over its shoulder as the opposition closed ground.

VI

Americans had done this before, but the standard of comparison had usually been our enemies, not our friends. In the fifties Russia's ability to orbit a satellite had prompted a tidal wave of nervous reflections. Then, the country's science and technology were said to be lagging. We needed more engineers, more physicists, more training in mathematics, more high-powered (meaning expensive) programs to explore space and master the physical universe. We rushed to develop new policies that would solve all of these problems and restore our supremacy. Later, when most of the programs had been successful, the fear wilted and many of the policies were abandoned. We had put our men on the moon. We apparently could concentrate then on other problems.

But in the seventies the comparisons were different both in quantity and quality, and we were less certain what the solutions should be. In Europe our postwar policy of strengthening the economies of the Western nations and of encouraging cooperation among their governments had been successful beyond all expectations. As the European Economic Community grew stronger, however, its members began to assert themselves more forcefully. The United States began to face tough competition from Europe, and the new balance of economic power was reflected in the declining value of the dollar. Early in the decade, the European central banks stopped supporting the value of the dollar. Foreign currencies were allowed to reach their market price relative to the U.S. dollar, and the result was a long downward slide in the value of our currency. This decline was merely one of the consequences of our new and somewhat diminished position in the world economy.

In the Far East the United States faced even more intense competition from Japanese companies. Here too the U.S. had helped a potential ally recover from the damage of World War II, only to find in Japan a powerful competitor for world markets. The yen increased in value relative to the dollar. While I would not claim that it was a major turning point in world history, I have my own personal measure of the shift that was taking place. I had learned to drive in a Chevrolet, and through most of my adult life I never drove any other type of car, let alone bought one. In 1978, however, I bought a Honda, as did 274,999 other Americans. The Japanese product was, in my studied opinion, far better built than comparable American cars. As more and more Americans reached this same conclusion, U.S. businessmen and bureaucrats and scholars began to look to Japan for models of how we might improve the efficiency and innovative nature of our industrial corporations.

In the Middle East, too, the balance of economic power shifted away from the U.S. The most significant development was the organization by the OPEC nations of an effective cartel. With the United States and its Western allies dependent upon supplies of crude oil from these countries, our policy alternatives were circumscribed. We could no longer manipulate these relatively weak governments as we had in the past. After the friendly regime we had helped bring to power in Iran was toppled in 1979, the United States could not play a forceful role in that country's internal affairs. There, as elsewhere, America was giving ground on the outer fringes of its empire. If it was any consolation, what the United States lost in this case could not be credited to Russia or its communist allies. The world had become more complex for them too. Russia (now having its own serious problems with China and with the Eastern European states) and the United States were both being forced to adjust to a world which could no longer be understood simply in terms of two opposing sides. That must have produced at least as much confusion and anxiety in the USSR as it did in the USA.

VII

In America at middle age, the feelings of impotence in the seventies thus had a real—in fact, a formidable—basis. We were not imagining these problems. Our difficulties were several and they involved the most basic institutions in our society. Our national system of fiscal and monetary controls had been badly misused. Our political leaders had seriously miscalculated the system's potential. Overseas and at home the United States had tried to do too much, and it was paying a price for overexertion. The severe inflation of the seventies made it especially difficult for the nation's nongovernmental organizations to respond creatively to the challenges they now faced at home and abroad. Our leadership at all levels of the society was suspect. From the boardrooms of our largest corporations to the Oval Office of the White House, America's leaders had in this decade blended ineptitude and corruption in a way that raised serious doubts about the future of this country.

It is difficult today to make a balanced appraisal of our strengths and weaknesses, standing as we are in the dark shadow of the seventies. Nevertheless, I would like to hazard a few tentative opinions about the state of our union at the end of that decade. One is that the widespread sense of impotence and anxiety was exaggerated. The American economy was still the most productive system in the world by a very wide margin. Our technology was on balance more advanced than that of any other nation. And our standard of living was the envy of the world; if we relaxed our restrictions on immigration, the rush of people to the U.S. would again provide testimony to the advantages of life in this country. Nor was our power in international affairs diminished so much as we felt it was in the aftermath of Vietnam. Possessed as we were of the terrible ability to destroy on short notice the cities and industries and military bases of almost any other nation, the United States was as yet a very toothy tiger. Even the dilemma provided by our leadership was not a hopeless situation. In politics and in the economy the United States was blessed with effective means of peacefully changing leaders. Thus, Chrysler, as well as the U.S. government, was able to put new men in charge without creating a major social trauma. For many other countries such transitions in power are very difficult to make without disruptive political struggles.

These assets notwithstanding, however, the problems of the United States were serious enough in the late seventies to suggest that the country was probably just entering the third phase in the evolution of its modern institutions. The first phase had involved the creation in the years between the late nineteenth century and about 1940 of a series of new and powerful organizations capable of promoting innovation and of protecting the income, status, and power of different groups in the society. By the 1940s a formidable array of such organizations wielded private and public power in this country. They assured that our system would remain innovative. They also helped protect people in the slower-growing, middle-aged society of this century. It became clear during the Great Depression, however, that their success hinged upon the aggregate performance of the economy. At that time, we still had no means of ensuring a satisfactory level of economic activity in the nation as a whole.

The second phase in the development of modern America began when we learned how to control the output of the world's most productive national economy. The quest had started in earnest during the 1930s, but the crucial period of institutional innovation was the 1940s. By the end of that decade, we had a new American system in place, armed with legal authority and a federal budget adequate to the task of manipulating the economy. We had the means now to keep America stable and prosperous. In the next thirty years we learned a great deal about what would and would not help us achieve those goals. In the seventies, in particular, we discovered how important good leadership and restraint were to this new set of institutions.

We began to enter the third phase of institutional change when the need for productivity-enhancing innovations became the central problem of the American system. No longer was the quest for security such a serious matter. In fact, there was reason to believe that America—like some cautious middle-aged men—had actually bought too much insurance. Our growth was being impaired by our inability to invest as we should in the means of achieving further technological and organizational progress. In a severely competitive international setting we could not afford to float, placidly enjoying our great wealth. We could not afford to cut our investments in research and development. We could not let our scientific and engineering establishments lag. But we did. We also could not afford the debilitating inflation generated by the public policies of the seventies. The price of these mistakes is evident in our sad record for growth in productivity.

To be successful in the third phase our public-sector performance—at all levels of government—surely will have to be improved. This crucial problem will probably be the most difficult one that Americans have encountered in this century. Triocracy is not a particularly flexible system of government. Also, we have no domestic tradition to guide us in dealing with this issue. Our conservatives have scorned government and our liberals have lauded it with equally thoughtless enthusiasm. Privatizing our bureaucracies will not succeed in the long run. We cannot make the Post Office successful by pretending it is General Motors (or Chrysler). It is not. Eighty years of experience with importing business executives to run our government agencies and departments on a temporary basis should have convinced us that they alone cannot bring about the transformation that is needed.

In fact the businesscrats may have had the opposite effect. One of the chief barriers to the solution to this problem has been the manner in which American values are weighted in favor of private enterprise. This discouraged the development of a tradition of public service and encouraged our public bureaucrats to build empires at the cost of good service to the public. Even worse, this mentality favored the sort of corruption that was so all-pervasive in the seventies. If the American way only involves making it, we must expect our public officials to continue to find plenty of feathers for their own nests.

Where can we look for help? Neither major party has much to say on this point, and none of the postwar pulses of political agitation have had anything positive to offer. All we can do is hope that politics, like nature, abhors a vacuum and that the years ahead will see the development of an appropriate ideology, elite, and supporting organizations. The White House might well provide some guidance. But since the crucial changes will have to start in Congress, that body might be the source of some fresh ideas and vigorous leadership. My own state of Maryland, which is blessed at this writing with two outstanding senators, might be the source of some bipartisan groundwork along these lines. If so, that would help me forget that Maryland's contribution to the sad decade of the seventies included Spiro T. Agnew.

9

SO WHAT?

So we recognize that the United States has changed in many important ways as it has become a middle-aged nation. What difference does it make to any of us? So what?

That harsh question deserves a prompt and straightforward answer. My reply is that the perspective you now have on America (if you skipped those early chapters to get to this conclusion, you should now go back and read them) will help you understand our country's past and present more fully and will enable you to do a better job of girding yourself properly for the battles ahead. This particular vision of a middle-aged society should also reassure you about the future, salving some of the worst anxieties aroused by recent events at home and abroad.

II

Since I am by trade a historian, let's first deal with the past. In my view, of course, the analysis and description presented in the previous chapters make more sense of our modern history than any of the alternatives with which I am familiar. For one thing, this perspective helps us to see how tightly interrelated were our foreign and domestic policies; our political and economic programs; the development of our business, farm, labor, and professional institutions—all of which evolved along somewhat similar lines. The entire society was drifting in one direction. Not toward collapse as radical critics would have it. Not toward the liberal's rendezvous with destiny. But toward middle age. Toward a new, complex, and highly durable institutional structure that itself would change dramatically the way most Americans lived. Toward a system of political economy that would make good leadership more important than it had ever been in the United States.

This vision of the past should also allow you to untangle some of the paradoxes in American history. Now you can see why a nation born in a great revolutionary war could become the leading antirevolutionary force in the world. You can understand why liberals in the 1970s were the fiercest opponents of some of the regulatory agencies that had themselves been liberal creations in an earlier day. You can reconcile the fact that more and more Americans have won the right to participate in our domestic politics with the fact that fewer and fewer of them bother to vote. Finally, you can explain now why our presidents in recent decades have come to preside over so much but have been able to change so little. They too have been captives of triocratic government, the polity of a middle-aged society.

III

This theme is also useful in interpreting the events of the present, including those awesome political struggles that have been taking place in Washington, D.C., since January 1981. The bugle call to battle in this case was our old friend the renewal symphony. President Reagan sounded the first loud note in his inaugural address and soon the strains could be heard echoing from Wall Street to the Golden Gate Bridge.

Time Inc. made American renewal a common theme of all its magazines, including *Fortune, Life, Sports Illustrated, Money, People,* and *Discovery,* as well as *Time.* As the publisher explained, the journals were all examining "what can be done to restore confidence in ourselves and our future" (*Time,* February 23, 1981). Intricate variations were played elsewhere. Discussing the space shuttle in *The New York Times Magazine,* John Noble Wilford exalted: "A people are testing themselves in relation to their heritage of steamboats, Conestoga wagons, railroads and airplanes, seeking reassurance that over the years the old vigor and resourcefulness have not left them" (April 5, 1981). Fortunately, after this much was put on the line, the space shuttle worked. But getting back to the "old vigor" proved, as it always does, to be a more elusive goal.

The most important step was to put tight reins on a national fiscal system that had broken out of control in the mid-sixties and had not been administered with proper restraint for fifteen years. The Reagan administration and a substantial majority of our representatives and senators recognized that federal spending and the deficit had to be reduced. The deficit-fueled inflation was undermining our most important economic institutions. At the national level our triocratic government had to be put on the fiscal equivalent of the Scarsdale diet, and the administration mounted an especially effective campaign to achieve this end. The difficulty of course was in determining exactly which programs would bear most of the reductions.

Every slice in the budget met determined resistance from deeply rooted interests. In a triocracy nothing is so difficult to accomplish as shrinking—let alone terminating—a well-defended program. Most of us became involved, either directly or indirectly, in these struggles. I wrote to my senators about the programs I treasured, the ones I felt should not be slimmed down. I contributed to the kitty used to finance various defensive campaigns. Many of you probably did the same through your associations, unions, clubs, or firms. If you were not this directly engaged, you can get a good sense of how tough these fights were merely by going back over the newspaper reports on the recent political activities of the dairy industry. Under direct attack from the administration, initially at least, the industry gave a bit of ground on one front, but then recovered all the lost territory and then some on the other front. This near-classic display of triocratic tactics was a success, despite the hostile environment the industry encountered on Capitol Hill. Other triumvirates were equally skillful, and even those that lost heavily in the first battle merely regrouped along their new lines, marshalling their clients and their clients' typewriters for the next phase of the war. Continuity of purpose is one of the hallmarks of triocracy.

What is most surprising, in fact, is the administration's initial degree of success in putting America on a fiscal diet. Clever political maneuvering and strong appealing leadership were essential to the effort. By cutting $35 billion of nondefense spending out of the budget, the Reagan forces won a substantial victory over triocracy. As this accomplishment suggests, our political situation is far from hopeless; we are not locked in, held forever on a course toward increased expenditures and deficits. Executives can promote conflict within the triocracies. They can use a blanket approach that averages the losses over large groups of interests, as the administration did in its first year. Triocracy is a very stable form of government, but it can be changed.

The second round of major cuts is just getting under way as these pages are being drafted, but already the likelihood of a similar victory in this phase (or future phases) of the campaign seems unlikely. In part this is because the triocracies have dug in, created new alliances, gathered additional financial resources, alerted the folks back home to the threat to their interests. In part, too, this political inertia is a result of other aspects of the Reagan program.

The tax-cut measure created a number of problems. It prevented the administration from reducing the deficit. Moreover, it was blatantly favorable to upper-income groups, highlighting the fact that most of the cuts in spending were being imposed on lower-income Americans. The welfare and educational programs that were slashed had served these groups and not the wealthy. The tax cuts for individuals and the embarrassing tax breaks for businesses were regressive measures that promised political problems for the administration if its programs did not quickly spur the national economy to higher levels of productivity, output, and employment. There was a threat too that the United States might suffer another outbreak of violence of the sort that struck our major cities in the sixties. The administration was racing against the clock and against those economic indicators that measure the success of our national system.

Continued deficits of major proportions, resulting from the tax cuts and heavy defense spending, promise to create more inflation and keep interest rates at a level that could eventually strangle many American businesses. There are now complaints that the Federal Reserve System is too worried about inflation and not worried enough about stimulating economic growth. But the history of the fifties and sixties strongly supports the Fed's version of what, exactly, should be accomplished first in controlling our national economy. Indeed, there is good reason for believing the Reagan administration was behaving like Sam the Marathon Man, trying to accomplish too much at once. The effort to reduce spending, cut taxes, lower the rate of inflation, and refurbish our national military establishment simultaneously may just be asking too much of a middle-aged society.

IV

If the present situation looks tenuous, what can we say about
the long-run future of America's new system of political economy? As our country enters the third phase of institution-
building, with its focus on enhancing productivity growth,
what should we expect? The historical perspective provided
in the previous chapters suggests that we should not expect
a great deal from one particular type of public policy: deregulation. From this viewpoint, you can predict that deregulation
of industry is more likely to produce significant short-term
than important long-run effects. Deregulation can indeed
have some beneficial results. These efforts, which began in
earnest in the 1970s, have in some cases already logged some
impressive accomplishments. By opening an industry to new
entrants (as in airlines) and by breaking down restrictive controls (as in trucking), deregulation has encouraged innovation
and growth. But as a result, we are not going to return to
the golden age of competition. You can jog away the fat but
not the years. These stabilizing arrangements—like thousands
of others—arose out of a new need for security and stability,
a need that could be and was met in a variety of ways, from
industry to industry, from occupation to occupation. Most
Americans, however, found some way to satisfy that need.
Deregulation, this outlook suggests, will do more to change
the form than it will to alter the long-run performance of
our economic organizations.*

*The same could be said about the interest in changing our social
security system in a major way. We all have a stake in keeping that system
solvent, and we all want to see it operated efficiently, with a minimum of
corruption. But we cannot today legislate away the needs that gave rise to
social security. The population and economic trends that generated the
demands for unemployment benefits, a retirement plan, and medical as-
sistance programs are alas beyond the control of even the United States
government.

Rather than spending the 1980s trying to chop all of the heads off the regulatory Hydra, we might do well to spend our energy looking for positive ways to meet the central challenge of this third phase in the history of our modern institutions. If we do, we will certainly want to do as much as we can to encourage the types of technological and organizational progress that will enhance our productivity. This problem needs all the attention we can give it. Again, our history helps us see some things that might be done. Agriculture in particular provides us with a useful model. The groundwork for the second agricultural revolution was laid in the decades before World War II, when federal and state programs built up a backlog of scientific and technological knowledge. In the 1940s, market forces in a competitive setting encouraged U.S. farmers to apply the new techniques, innovating along lines that greatly enhanced the efficiency of our agricultural sector. We should recognize that our federal policies of production and price control did not prevent these changes from taking place. We should also remember that the state and federal programs involving support for scientific research and technical innovation did not pay off until many decades after they had been started. Patience is as important to our middle-aged society as it is to the forty-year-old, weekend athlete.

America's record of accomplishment in agriculture indicates that we should now be doing everything we can afford to build up our scientific and engineering establishments. In an intensive economy facing severe competition from overseas, anything less than this is foolhardy. On balance the United States still appears to have a technological edge on most of the world's other industrial powers. But since the late sixties we have been allowing our investments in research and development to lag. The federal government is no longer supporting basic research as it did in the fifties and early sixties. Meanwhile, the great inflation appears to have constrained R & D expenditures by private firms. It would be shortsighted to allow either of those trends to continue.

It would also be dangerous to ignore any longer the need to improve our public sector's performance. This, we can be certain, will be the most difficult of the third phase problems to solve. We have in recent decades charged our several governments with many new and important responsibilities. But we have given little thought to what can be done to ensure that these public institutions have innovative leaders and efficient administrations. We have allowed our government agencies and departments to drift into triocratic alliances which have dramatically changed the nature of our polity. We would do well at this point to worry a bit less about how much money to give these public institutions and to worry a bit more about how well they do with the resources they already control.

In foreign as in domestic policy America at middle age will need prudent leaders who are mindful of the limits of our military and economic power. The contrast between what we accomplished in the fifties and what we lost in the following decades deserves some attention from all those who want to see the United States take a more forceful position in the world today. The U.S. will have to be realistic about its resources and about its priorities abroad if it is to avoid the sort of debilitating encounter we experienced in Vietnam. America cannot protect its vital interests in Europe and Latin America if it is bogged down in fruitless attempts to thwart every national socialist revolution on the frontiers of our empire.

If we are realistic, we will all demand less from our foreign policy than we have in the past. We should forget about making the United States the examplar, the so-called "city on a hill," that provides all other nations with the model they should emulate. What an awful burden to carry. We should instead be satisfied when the United States uses its wealth and power skillfully to seek its own carefully circumscribed objectives. We cannot avoid using our power. Nor can we avoid being the enemy of change. But we can exercise our power with great care, recognizing that the enemies of today can be the friends of the future, as has so often been the case in the past.

If we do so, a reasonable appraisal of our accomplishments in this century indicates that we have good grounds to be optimistic about the future. America's record is impressive. The transition from a fast-growing, extensive society to a modern, intensive system was demanding. The most basic of our economic institutions had to be transformed, as did our polity. We developed great modern organizations that provided us with security and also ensured that the U.S. would remain innovative. To our credit, we came through this transition in a relatively peaceful manner, emerging with most of our basic freedoms intact. Moreover, the United States has continued to grow, although at a more sedate pace, and has continued to change in ways that invite our calm, mature respect.

Most of us actually like ourselves better at middle age than we did when we were younger. I certainly do. Perhaps that's why I am so optimistic about the middle years of our society. The United States is a highly creative country which has contributed much to the world's music, art, and literature in this century. Our scientists have excelled. Our humanists have made great advances in scholarship. Our economic system is the most productive, by far, of any in existence today. Our political system still gives each of us a commendable freedom of choice and a reassuring freedom from fear. As citizens of this wealthy, accomplished, and powerful nation, we all have the right to enjoy America at middle age.

ACKNOWLEDGMENTS

Like the Beatles, I get by with the help of my friends. Some of them give me money, others the kinds of things money can't buy: their intelligence, interest, affection, respect, encouragement, tolerance. You know what I mean. All of those things that help you finish a book.

In this case I started writing the manuscript when I was on a Senior Fellowship from the National Endowment for the Humanities. Now, as I complete these pages, the Endowment is one of those government agencies in the budget battles I have described. I am in the coils of my own history, describing triocracy one minute, playing the role of client the next—writing to my congressmen, sending checks to my interest group to support our lobby, trying to keep alive the programs that have served me so well. Without the Endowment's support and the free time it provided, there would be no book. What else can I say on behalf of NEH?

During that year of leave, my family had to put up with me grumping around the house. I hope they know how much I appreciate their tolerance. They didn't choose to spend that much time around an author. It just happened.

Once the writing was under way, there was typing and

copying and retyping and more copying and mailing to be done. These several chores were done with a smile (and an occasional helpful comment on my chapters) by Deborah Lewis, Bożena Lamparski, James Higgs, and Betty Paynter. Betty Whilden directed the traffic, and Janet Seraphine typed all of the last draft, under pressure of a tight deadline.

When a complete draft was finished, a number of my friends took the time to read and comment on the manuscript. I stole their good ideas with relish. The victims of this thievery included Bitsie Clark, John Phelps Clark, Daun van Ee, Robert Gallman, Robert Garnet, Philip B. Haff, Robert Hogan, Betty Hughes, Ben Josephson, Kenneth S. Lynn, Sue Martin, Thomas W. Murray, Joe Pratt, and Maurice Bessman. Even my clever agent, Gerard McCauley, got into this act (as he did later when it came time to sell the final product). If the book is not perfect after receiving all of this attention, the man whose name is on the title page is clearly at fault.

He certainly cannot blame his academic setting for his flaws. The Johns Hopkins University is, hands down, the best place in the United States to do this kind of work. My colleagues, my chairman, my students, both undergraduate and graduate—even my dean, my provost, and my president all contributed in special ways to this endeavor.

Along the way toward the final printed pages, I was helped by two research assistants. I am grateful to the intrepid Israeli Avi Zakai for starting the job. The bulk of the manuscript was completed with the skillful and enthusiastic support of C. T. Marcinko. To all of these friends, my thanks.

Index